About the Author

When Alexandra was pole-axed with depression she looked for ways to help herself recover without resorting to prescription drugs. Once fully recovered she began to help others by counselling and working on telephone support lines. In 2004 Alexandra published the first of her many books. She is a passionate champion for those who still suffer.

www.alexandramassey.co.uk

Alexandra Massey

Beat Depression Fast

Ten Steps to a Happier You

WATKINS PUBLISHING
LONDON

This edition first published in the UK and USA 2014 by
Watkins Publishing Limited
PO Box 883
Oxford, OX1 9PL
UK

A member of Osprey Group

For enquiries in the USA and Canada:
Osprey Publishing
PO Box 3985
New York, NY 10185-3985
Tel: (001) 212 753 4402
Email: info@ospreypublishing.com

1 3 5 7 9 10 8 6 4 2

Edited and typeset by Donald Sommerville

Printed and bound by CPI Group (UK) Ltd, Croydon, CR0 4YY

A CIP record for this book is available from the British Library

ISBN: 978-1-78028-605-1

Watkins Publishing is supporting the Woodland Trust, the UK's leading
woodland conservation charity, by funding tree-planting initiatives and woodland
maintenance.

www.watkinspublishing.co.uk

Publisher's Note

The information in this book is not intended as a substitute for professional
medical advice and treatment. If you are pregnant or are suffering from any
medical conditions or health problems, it is recommended that you consult a
medical professional before following any of the advice or practice suggested
in this book. Watkins Publishing Ltd., or any other persons who have been
involved in working on this publication, cannot accept responsibility for any
injuries or damage incurred as a result of following the information, exercises or
therapeutic techniques contained in this book.

Contents

Introduction

This is a book for those people who have suffered from depression but haven't been able to find the way out. It's for people who've suffered from depression for weeks, months or years – as I have. It's written as a guide to a journey that we need to take if we want to beat depression *fast* and *for good*.

Some within the medical profession say that depression is simply a result of a chemical imbalance in the brain. However, if, like me, you've taken anti-depressants and not found them to be the answer over the long term, you'll know that beating depression is not so simple as popping a pill. I don't deny that anti-depressants may be necessary for some people in certain stages of severe depression. But through my own experiences I have discovered that depression goes way beyond the simplistic description of a chemical imbalance. Depression is an emotional illness which drains life out of the sufferer and its legacy is to leave them feeling helpless, hopeless and defeated. In this book I want to introduce you to the steps you can take to tackle depression when it strikes and protect yourself against its reappearance. I know these steps work because I've been down this road too.

Can I really beat depression fast?

The new science of Positive Psychology is showing us how to beat depression fast. We no longer need to lie back on the couch, discuss our history and go over and over the past. Our past is only a mental story and spending long periods of time trying to work out what went wrong keeps the story alive. When we keep our story alive it simply increases the depression and our powerlessness because there is nothing we can do about it.

Although we can't change what happened in the past we can transform our lives today with the skills we have right now. Regardless of what happened in the past, we can learn to bring our awareness into the present moment so that struggles, problems, unhappiness and depression dissolve. They can be replaced with a sense of peace and acceptance of what happened in the past. We can use this new Positive Psychology to quickly transform the way we view our past story, use the steps to move us away from a negative life and help us to build a strong future

My story

I had suffered from depression since my childhood, although I didn't recognize it as depression until much later in my life. My mother always told me that I'd ruined her life and, as a result, I felt I was the 'problem' child. I spent my childhood trying to be a good girl to make my mother happy but I never discovered what it was I had to do to please her. I grew up thinking there was 'something wrong with me'. I spent my teen years getting into trouble but I was actually trying to run from my pain. By the time I reached my early twenties I was extremely depressed. However, I soon discovered the joy of workaholism and spending the monthly pay check in the sales. I'd finally found something that could 'numb' me out so I didn't have to feel the round-the-clock awfulness of the dark emotions I was trying to escape from. Of course, the world gives its thumbs up to anyone who works hard so there was no reason to stop. For several years I worked 14-hour days, spent money like it was going out of fashion, travelled the world, shopped in Bond Street, owned property, cars and sponsored a motor racing team! But by the time I turned 30 I'd crashed and burned and suffered an emotional breakdown.

For three years I was unable to work, or even function because I was pole-axed with chronic depression. I looked everywhere for help but it wasn't easy to find. All doctors could offer at the time were anti-depressants, but I needed so much more. In the end I joined a self-help group, signed up for meditation classes, started eating more healthily, read lots of books and tried some counselling. However, I spent a lot of time stumbling around without much direction and the things that worked were self-taught. My first book, *Beat Depression and Reclaim Your Life*, was the result of my own journey. It was a guide to help sufferers through a series of steps that looked at the past and helped them to move out of the depression by challenging old patterns largely seated in childhood.

This book is different because it looks at the ways to beat depression *faster* by adopting the essence of Positive Psychology. I wish I'd known about these techniques when I was suffering because it would have got me back on my feet quicker. These new concepts are interpretations of old ideas – but the results of recent studies are bringing them onto the medical radar. For example, one study, published in the journal *Frontiers in Human Neuroscience* in February 2013, reported that mindfulness meditation, an important element of Positive Psychology, can cut the recurrence of depression by 50%. That is an incredible figure, which no pharmaceutical can match. We are seeing the beginning of a radical re-think in the way that depression is managed. Studies such as these are breaking new ground and setting the pace for a much-needed change within the medical world.

The new world of Positive Psychology

Positive Psychology is a whole new approach to emotional well-being that has been initiated in just the last ten years and is quickly gathering pace. It's the scientific study of the strengths and virtues that enable people to thrive as opposed to the study of what's wrong with us. It points towards taking on board what makes us happy rather than trying to figure out all the things that need to be mended. It explains that it's not about fixing the problem but rather a matter of understanding and accepting the problem so that our natural resilience and healing helps us to get back to peace and happiness. There are some magnificent writers making waves in this new field like Eckhart Tolle, Robert Holden,

Barbara Fredrickson, Martin Seligman and Steven C Hayes. Oxford University has devoted a whole department to studying this new thinking and is spreading the word about mindfulness, transcending thought and raising personal awareness.

The world of psychology has been heavily influenced by Sigmund Freud, the father of psychoanalysis. Many modern theories of the human psyche have developed from his work. His theories served as the foundation for a school of psychology that quickly rose to become a dominant force during its early years. His main premise was that our parents had everything to do with the way we view life as adults and that our childhood wasn't just influential, it could dominate our adult selves. Although Freud's theories are highly controversial, they are still also highly influential. Until now, that is. Positive Psychology is challenging that influence and suggesting that it is possible to recover from depression without having to spend months or years on the couch. Freud died in 1939 yet, since then, the rates of depression have increased ten-fold. Dr Martin Seligman, a distinguished experimental psychologist, was quoted in the American Psychological Association journal *Monitor* in October 1988 that people born after 1945 were ten times more likely to suffer from depression than people born 50 years earlier. This suggests that these old ways of looking at depression haven't worked as well as they should.

The World Health Organization on depression

If you are depressed, take heart, you are not alone. The World Health Organization (WHO) states that by 2030 depression will be the leading cause of ill-health worldwide. Depression is called the 'silent killer' because the shame that surrounds sufferers often prevents them from getting help. However, things are changing and the WHO also states that depression is no longer thought of as a 'self indulgence', with sufferers who should 'pull their socks up', but is recognized as a real threat to emotional, mental and physical health. Those of us who've suffered know exactly what that means.

How this book can help

My aim is to take you on a journey of self-discovery and understanding that will help you to beat depression fast. I will explain why we get depressed as well as offer guidance, through ten steps, to climb out. These insights helped me to understand my depression and I discovered that, once I understood why I was stuck, it was much easier to climb out of the black hole. It also prevented me from falling back in so often. There's no point in trying for a temporary reprieve. Although I've been grateful when the depression lifted, before I practised mindfulness I always feared its return. But now this has changed. I no longer have depressive episodes so I know it can be beaten for good. However, it wasn't easy. I had to do a lot of 'work'. By this I mean committing to my recovery, taking it seriously, eating better food, becoming more assertive, doing exercises and practising meditation. It was a bit like going to the gym and working out. I knew the result I wanted but I also knew I had to put in the time. This is what I mean by work. The exercises provided in this book are what I practise day in day out, especially the meditations. They are what keep me level, balanced and happy. I no longer fear the depression returning.

There is a linear path to this book; it starts at the beginning by showing you how to stop fighting the depression through acceptance and then how to release the feelings that are buried deep inside. It will take you by the hand and show you how to let go, trust yourself and guide you to meet your hidden self – your inner child. I explain how your internal loving parent can help you reconnect with your inner child. Healing toxic shame will help you to mend the broken pieces of your shattered self. You will discover new power as you take responsibility for your emotional well-being and discover your true self, without the depression. By stilling the mind you will find peace and by learning more about 'Bodywork' you will understand how the depression has affected your body and uncover practical ways to make yourself feel better, faster. Finally, you will discover what to do to cultivate long-lasting happiness.

PART ONE

Starting Out

CHAPTER 1

All About Depression

*What 'being depressed' means
to someone who is suffering*

I've had many letters from people who've been depressed and I find that knowing I'm not alone has helped me a great deal. Here are are just a few that you, too, may find helpful. I have changed the names.

> My depression is at a level now that I feel . . . lifeless; probably that's the best way to describe it. I have no energy, feel numb and as if I'm in a dream every day. I hate myself for being like this. I feel a lot of pain (not physical, well, not always) even with just thinking. It's all I do. Think about the past . . . I don't enjoy life. I never have. Happiness is another thing I don't understand. It's foreign to me. I feel like an empty shell. No emotion any more. The only feeling is pain. I see no way forward. *Mike*

> I feel like the most hated person in the world at the moment, my self-esteem is at an all time low. I often feel that if I wasn't here nobody would be bothered. I am very tearful and have been in the supermarket doing my weekly shop and nearly burst into tears. I am a very nervous person and lack confidence. I am praying that

there will be a light at the end of the tunnel, I hate the feeling that everyone hates me at work. I'm thinking of looking for another job so I don't have to go back and face anyone. *Sharon*

I feel so messed up! I feel like I'm trapped in a bubble, I feel so lonely, tearful and don't want to face anyone. When my family are around I have to act as normal as I can as I don't want to put any worries on them. I have to walk out of the room and weep as I don't want them worrying. *Richard*

I have suffered from very bad mood swings all my life but now they are taking over. One day I will be in the best mood ever and want to do erratic things like work abroad and the next I am so down I think about suicide. I am pushing my family away but not intentionally. It's got to a point where my own mum is afraid to talk to me because she doesn't know how I will react, whether I will be nice or completely flip out. *Deborah*

I am petrified to speak to a doctor. How are you supposed to tell them you don't know what's wrong with you? I feel embarrassed. I have huge barriers up against everyone. People think I am a lovely bubbly person but a smile can hide everything. *Vicky*

What is depression?

Wikipedia defines depression as a 'state of low mood'. Whoa! Has anyone at Wikipedia ever suffered from depression? Obviously not!

Depression can be described as a state of low mood *only at its very best*. I will describe what depression was like for me; maybe this will resonate for you, too. Depression was a life-sapper, an end of life as I knew it. Depression began to tear away piece by piece my hopes and dreams, deconstructing my ability to maintain good relationships and creating a helplessness and hopelessness of the very, very deepest kind. It manifested itself as a dark, brooding cloud that settled on my chest and moved its way up and down until it filled the whole cavity of my existence so that I couldn't see further than my nose. It then took me down into a bottomless black pit into which no light could enter and from where there seemed no escape. It robbed me of my self-esteem and all motivation to change. It found ways of telling me how useless I'd been in the past and told me that there was no hope for the future.

Once I'd reached the bottom of the pit the depression told me that I was worth nothing more. Then it positively encouraged self-hate to the point where I acted out to stop the pain. In my case I became a workaholic, but there are lots of different tools to try: for some people it may be drugs, smoking, alcoholic bingeing, spending money they don't have, self-harm, dangerous sexual relationships, sugar and junk food bingeing, acting-out violence, abusiveness and self-neglect.

The cycle of depression and self-harm

Depression – self-hate – self-harm – more depression –
more self-hate – more self-harm – more depression.

The more we hate ourselves for feeling depressed, the more we act out to try to stop the pain by indulging in behaviour which perpetuates the depression and causes more pain. It becomes an endless loop.

Why are we depressed?

For the last 70 years, the world of psychology has been obsessed with the idea of 'mental illnesses'. Billions, no trillions, of pounds have been invested into trying to find out why we suffer this 'disorder' in such large numbers and why the rates of 'mental illness' are soaring phenomenally. Depression has been sub-categorized into new 'illnesses' such as melancholic depression, bipolar depression, dysthymic disorder, major depression, post-partum depression and seasonal affective disorder. There are at least 14 'mental illnesses', all of which have a corresponding medication blueprint of 'effective treatment'. The truth is that in spite of all the money spent on research, no medical authority can confidently answer the basic question: Why are so many of us depressed?

As a person who has recovered from depression this is my answer. Depression happens when we deny our real, authentic selves. It's the psyche's way of dealing with situations that we find difficult or maybe impossible to manage. It's what happens when we can't stand up for ourselves and use our natural resources to move on. It's what overcomes us when we have lost sight of our dreams or when we can't see a way to escape from a tight spot. Depression settles on our soul when we have given up on ourselves. It's like a blanket that numbs out the pain but in the process it also numbs out the joy.

The two-pronged attack

Depression affects us in two critical ways: first, it presses down emotions and second, it makes us over-think. Let's look at each of these in turn.

Not expressing emotions healthily

The very word 'de-pressed' suggests that something is being held down. We are depressed because we have pushed down emotions that we can't allow to come to the surface. We constantly experience a range of emotions; how we handle them determines the level of our emotional health. If we feel angry but don't express that anger in a healthy way, we will either act it out in ways that might be harmful to us, or we will ignore it and 'de-press' it. If we feel sad but don't let it out, we hold back the tears until they are also 'de-pressed down'.

Over-thinking

Over-thinking is the second thing that makes us depressed. What is over-thinking? Another term for it is rumination. It's the tendency to go over and over things in the mind like a record that's stuck in a groove and keeps repeating the same sequence. It's replaying an argument or retracing past mistakes in an obsessive way. Research has found that this habit makes us emphasize the negative things that happened to us in the past and interpret situations in our current lives more negatively. We become so preoccupied with our problems that we're unable to push past the negative thoughts.

We all face adversity and the way we deal with it was taught to us as children. When our life is going well, we don't question the way we tick. But when we hit a bad patch, if we don't have a compassionate, in-built method of dealing with life's messiness and, by default, we ignore our natural response, we can easily fall into a depressive state. We weren't born depressed (unless our mother was addicted to alcohol or a drug that requires going through lengthy withdrawal symptoms and this didn't happen to most of us) so something happened to us to start the depression. Part of the recovery from depression is finding out what happened so we can change it.

Depression needs our help to hang around

The strange thing about depression is if we let it take its natural course we would recover in good time. Depression is a temporary state. If we let our natural resilience move us through the process, we would come out the other side and recover. Generally we don't accept the depression as a part of a natural cycle and we try to outrun it. But in trying to outrun it, we make it bigger than it needs to be.

Depression is both socially unacceptable and painful. We do things to try and keep it away from us. We try to escape it by 'getting on' with our lives. It's called 'running on empty' – we try to keep ourselves going although we don't have enough fuel to do so. Because we feel like emotional cripples, we have to use crutches to keep us going. We 'numb' our feelings with high sugar/fat food, alcohol, cigarettes, work, shopping, compulsive sex or exercise, drugs or anything else that's going to keep us functioning at some level. It's easy to find ways of keeping the lid on our emotions. If we do this for long enough, depression becomes 'normal'.

Once we're stuck in the day-to-day blackness, it can seem

impossible to find a way out. Instead of outrunning the depression, somehow it has overtaken and outrun us.

Seeing depression another way: how it can help us

When all else fails, depression can feel like a comfort blanket. At least we know what it is and we know that when we're in a full bout of depression we can give up on ourselves. If you've suffered from depression for a long time, it can become a 'default position'. It can seem comforting to return to that hopeless, helpless place when life feels too hard and messy. When I was in this state I understood the mess I was getting myself into when I gave up and sank back into the pit of depression; but there were benefits . . . better the devil you know, I thought! And because 'hopelessness' is one of the pillars of depression, I also felt hopeless about ever recovering from it, which kept me locked in the depression cycle.

But what if the depression you're suffering can actually help you? In the same way that physical pain signals an injury which needs to be treated, depression can signal some life changes which need to be put in place. If you feel your knee is hurting it can mean you need to take a break from your running workout and rest up until it recovers. Likewise, suffering from depression can mean that something in your life isn't working or that you need to take a step back and re-assess what needs to be addressed. What important advantages could the depression be conferring?

Being depressed certainly backs you into a corner but here you may also discover solitude, time and space. It might be taking you away from distressing or futile situations and allowing a little breathing space. This pause offers you a chance to take a fresh view on life and perhaps prevents you from making rash decisions or gives you time to re-assess relationships.

Certainly, for me, tackling the depression took me to a new place. Obviously I felt better because I recovered from the depressive symptoms, but the process also transformed me. The depression signalled that something was seriously wrong and needed working through and then changing. I was able to break out of a mould that had been imposed on me. It helped me discover who I truly was, which added much more meaning to my life. From the pit of depression I was able to find that deep space which increased my creativity and purpose. I could see that I wasn't a failure but I'd taken on too much and something inside said 'enough is enough'.

The depression looked after me while I was able to explore the reasons why I was trying to fight the world. I could have swept the turmoil under the carpet and carried on up the career ladder but it was the depression that helped me to lie low. It taught me to take care of the important things in life – good relationships, self-love, living in today, and developing compassion. I became more honest and truthful, especially to myself. I had to find courage to face some of these life truths, like how much I wanted to control those around me (probably the hardest bit of the journey) and also how much I relied on others to give me a sense of self-worth – such a painful place to be!

If I'd not had the courage to find my own way through depression and I'd gone down the medical route, I would have believed I was simply suffering from a chemical imbalance in my brain. This would have been a disservice to me. I knew that popping a pill was not the answer. I would never have had the opportunities to recognize and address life-changing problems or the chance to fulfil my potential or to have the appreciation of the world around me I do now.

CHAPTER 2

How This Book Can Help to Beat Depression *Fast*

Psychologists and psychiatrists have been telling us for 150 years that the way to beat depression is to find out *what's wrong with you*. We blindly followed this theory until the start of the 21st century when the idea was mooted that, instead, why don't we purposefully pursue *happiness*? Within a short time funds were being pumped into research and now we have Positive Psychology. The proponents of Positive Psychology argued that not only could you increase your happiness levels but you could also increase the lastingness of your happiness levels. They said that you could increase the range of your positive emotions and that this would override depressive traits.

This new insight into human emotions has grown faster than any other branch of psychology. There are two reasons: we all want to be happy, and it works. Positive Psychology guides us towards the light and helps us by giving us hope that we can feel better. But the principles of this approach are not new: the ethos and values have been advocated by spiritual teachers for thousands of years and centre around the importance of good relationships, finding meaning and purpose in daily life, cultivating compassion and gratitude, contributing to the greater good, savouring the present moment, achieving a sense of accomplishment, and reframing difficult events as opportunities for growth.

A word of caution: Positive Psychology is not a simplistic, instantaneous cure-all. We can't afford to mix this up with 'positive thinking', which means trying to see everything in an optimistic light. Positive Psychology is about *self-healing* as opposed to having someone else tell us what is wrong with us. Working with this approach is more of a flowing journey down a river than a tick-box exercise with a psychologist. It's a way of harnessing your awareness to bring about change in the present moment. If you've been depressed for a long time, it offers ways to help you feel better faster, even if you can't get in touch with your inner self, or you're numbed out and unable to feel your feelings, or you don't know what's wrong with you. Even if you think you're beyond help and you'll never get better, you can and you will

The heart of Positive Psychology:
Mindfulness & acceptance

We live in exciting times. New technologies to scan brains are accumulating evidence showing that sustained contemplation and meditation can actually bring about physical changes in brain structures associated with the experience of well-being and peace and ease of mind. Science is telling us that Positive Psychology is working. In this book we focus on the two beating hearts of Positive Psychology: mindfulness and acceptance.

Mindfulness

Mindfulness is the awareness that emerges through purposefully paying attention to the present moment. By cultivating a mindful approach to depression we can discover how to live in the present moment rather than obsessing about the past or worrying about the future. Mindfulness is an age-old concept based on Buddhist practices which originated perhaps about 2,600 years ago. It has been referred to as a 'psychological state of awareness without judging'. It's a combination of slowing down, doing one activity at a time and bringing full awareness both to our inner experience and to our outer activity. It provides a potentially powerful antidote to the stress of time-pressures, self-imposed expectations, overload, distraction, agitation and worry. Mindfulness is a state of mind, not a behavioural trait and, even though it might be promoted by certain practices or activities such as tai chi, it is not equivalent to or synonymous with them.

Mindfulness helps us to uncover a new sense of assurance and self-confidence. Through regular practice we become mindful of our emotions, their impact, their causes, and their impermanence. We become mindful toward our own thinking processes. We become aware of how certain thoughts affect our emotions. We learn how to take a step back, assess the results and then respond in a fully mindful way. We become an impartial witness to our thoughts and experiences as they come and go. The more we practise mindfulness, the more we are able to overcome the constant self-judging and over-reacting to inner and outer experiences that constantly stream through our minds. Eventually, we develop sustained concentration and can uncover new perspectives, gain greater insight and unleash creative problem-solving.

Mindfulness is developed by practising 'mindfulness meditation'. Mindfulness meditation is a self-regulating practice that focuses on training the attention and awareness to bring the mind under greater voluntary control and thereby create general emotional well-being, calmness, clarity and concentration. Studies carried out at Oxford University have shown that, not only does mindfulness meditation help relieve depression symptoms fast, it can also cut the recurrence of depression by a massive 50%.

Mindfulness has been adopted in Silicon Valley amongst other industries. Steve Jobs credited mindfulness as having helped him to tune out distractions when he needed to focus on building Apple. Google has been offering mindfulness training to its employees for five years and has a programme called 'Search Inside Yourself' to help Google's top brains relax and calm down. Its aim is to help employees build inner joy while they work. How cool is that! The course has five hundred on the waiting list!

Mindfulness and depression

There is a very logical reason that explains why mindfulness can help to pull us out of depression. When we feel depressed, our instinct is either to ignore the depression or 'think' our way out of it. In trying to think our way out of the depression we end up going over and over the past or obsessing about the future, all in an effort to take us away from the painful feelings going on now. Of course, neither of these tactics works, so we end up feeling even more stuck and then beat ourselves up for failing to find a solution. As the internal dialogue heats up, we become preoccupied with the battle we've got inside our heads and we lose touch with the reality of our world, the people who surround us, and the help that's available. We begin to feel hopeless. The depression is taking us over and we can't see a way out of it – and the despair begins to set in.

Mindfulness can break this cycle by helping us to take a completely new approach. It's a way of helping to stop our minds obsessing about the past and the future. The real value is being able to step out of the reaction we're having to a situation, which is usually automatic or by reflex, so we can do something different. By practising mindfulness on a regular basis, studies have shown that it's possible to get some control over the racing mind, stop focusing on the regrets of the past, and stop worrying about the future.

Mindfulness-based cognitive therapy

Mindfulness-Based Cognitive Therapy, or MBCT, is the fairly recently developed psychological approach to help people specifically suffering from depression. It uses traditional therapy methods but weaves in mindfulness, meditation and acceptance. The cognitive part includes looking at why we're depressed and helps to educate us. Its theory says that when individuals who have historically had depression become distressed, they return to automatic processes that can trigger a depressive episode. The aim of MBCT is to interrupt these automatic processes that drag us back to our 'default' learned behaviour. It then teaches us to focus less on reacting to incoming stimuli, instead accepting and observing them without judgement. The mindfulness part allows us to notice when automatic processes are occurring and to alter our responses to be more reflective.

This fits in with my story and those of thousands of others who've been through the traditional approaches of therapy/anti-depressants/group work and have found they've not done the job. Although other approaches can work, they don't always work fast enough and they don't always stick. Before I embraced mindfulness I found that unless I had someone on tap to talk to whenever I had negative thoughts and feelings, I wouldn't be able to function properly; but having someone constantly on tap was never a realistic scenario. I would automatically return to my 'default' position when the going got tough. Since I started practising mindfulness that pattern has changed. I now know I have a central core of solid support within myself which I can turn to *any time I want*! For someone who's suffered from depression for a long time, it's a life-saver because, for the first time, I feel confident that I can stay with, and accept, any emotions that I experience. The relief of knowing this is, some days, enough to make me punch the air; it really is that powerful!

The alternative to fixing and magnifying negative events would be to *distract* myself from them by doing something different to try to escape from them. The problem with this is that, consistent with the literature of avoiding negative thoughts, the more we try to escape from them the more prevalent they become to dominate our thinking.

MBCT is described as the 'third wave' of behavioural therapies. We've had the mind and the emotions and now the third wave is bringing in wisdom. Wisdom means *making space for events, thoughts and emotions instead of reacting to them*. In mainstream CBT practitioners use the term 'magnification', which suggests we make our thoughts into something much bigger than they actually are. In MBCT we bring in the wise mind, which allows thoughts, emotions and events to be *as they are*. This stops magnification and inner conflict in their tracks.

Acceptance

Acceptance is the acknowledgement of what's going on inside us and a willingness to be with it in this present moment. 'Acknowledge and allow' is the simple way of understanding acceptance. Acceptance helps us to get in touch with a deeper sense of ourselves that we can't reach when our minds are racing or when we're trying to ignore our despair. This deep self is known as the transcendent self, the part of us that holds wisdom – the wisdom that knows there is something beyond the limits of our feelings, thoughts and depression.

We don't have to like an experience to accept it. But resisting it will make it seem bigger. For example, by judging a certain situation as 'bad' or 'unpleasant', it can make the experience much bigger than it needs to be. There's a well-known saying: what you resist persists. Resisting, like pushing wet sand, is exhausting and achieves nothing. Another way of expressing the idea is by the equation: pain x resistance = suffering, which implies that if we want to alleviate suffering we can either reduce the pain or the resistance. Here's the shortcut: practise acceptance to alleviate the pain!

To give you an example, if someone cancels a date and I feel disappointed, I can either let my mind run into a negative feedback loop or distract myself by immediately fixing a date with someone else, which is trying to escape from the negativity by 'fixing it'. Alternatively, I could accept it, and in doing so, let the internal conflict go – poof, like sand in the wind.

Accepting a difficult feeling doesn't mean that we have to feel that way for ever or that we will be passive and not take action that might be needed. Acceptance means to become more aware of the reality of 'what is' in the present moment. Being more open and honest with the present moment creates the possibility of healing it faster and with compassion. For example, accepting a depressive feeling and perhaps writing about it, instead of trying to push it away, will help to take the 'sting' out of the depression and make it seem more bearable.

It's like releasing the pressure from an over-inflated tyre: the ride will soften and jarring decrease and the journey will become more manageable. Self-judging will lessen, which automatically lifts the shame. Bringing acceptance into our lives also helps to build a safe harbour that we can access and return to. Each time that we work through a difficulty, we release the grip of depression and its accompanying hopelessness. In time, love and self-awareness grow to establish personal freedom.

Coming into the 'here and now'

Mindfulness and acceptance both help to gather up our attention and escort it into the 'here and now'. Bringing ourselves into this literally breathtaking space can help clear away the negativity that surrounds us when we're in a full depressive episode. The idea is that by being in the present moment we are better able to experience the reality of our lives rather than give significance to our re-creation of the past and our unknown future. This can help us to alleviate current distress and hopelessness, which will give us the breathing space we need to take stock and fulfil our potential as a loving person who is simply depressed.

Being in this space is at the heart of healing from depression – *fast*. It helps us to mop up past regrets and calm the frantic mind which focuses on a desolate future. It helps us to discover that we are part of something bigger and we can connect to it. It helps us to recover from distress and teaches us how to get a profound perspective on life that stays with us even when we experience the peaks and troughs. Once we have discovered how easy it is to get into this space through mindfulness and acceptance, we have the tools to achieve our potential as warm, excited, happy, whole human beings.

By staying in the present moment we will also gain a better understanding of how our minds, feelings and bodies are connected. In 'Bodywork' we explore the synergy between these three parts of us and learn how to acknowledge these patterns so that we can move beyond a knee-jerk reaction, instead becoming more measured in how we respond to people and circumstances. In uncovering our inner child we learn to understand the part of us that is hurting. As we discover our wisdom we can allow the healing to begin.

This acceptance will help us understand that the answer lies within us and that we have the power to help ourselves move from hurting to healing and on to a free and fulfilling life.

CHAPTER 3

Preparing for Recovery

You may have had many failed attempts at trying to beat depression. I certainly had times when I thought 'Yay, that's it, I'm better' only to find that a few days later I was feeling like the worm that lives in a cow pat; what the hell happened to put me back into that hole? It takes an understanding of the recovery path to be able to see the bumps in the road.

Three phases of recovery

One thing you may find helpful is to know that the path of recovery comes in three phases. The **first phase** consists of alleviating the worst of the depression symptoms so you feel safer within yourself and in your environment. The **second phase** is to explore the reasons for your depression and challenge them so that the fear and confusion are removed. And the **third phase** is to reconnect with your inner self and important others you may have lost touch with whilst the depression 'took you away'. Rebuilding close relationships will help you build a bridge back to a sense of wholeness and purpose.

Finding support

You may need extra help to get through these phases. In preparing for recovery you may want to identify some people you could talk to. These must be people who offer a safe house for your thoughts and feelings. Whether you find a counsellor, a supportive group or an organization that can be there for you, what counts is that you will not be judged for what you say or criticized for how you feel. Friends are great but it may be worth seeking out others who will know how you feel. There is a list of resources in *How to Get Help* at the end of the book.

Journalling

Writing is a brilliant way of helping to speed up recovery from depression. Studies show that writing acts as a shock absorber against excessive thinking, which is something we all do when we're depressed. Writing, instead of thinking, helps to get problems out of the mind and onto paper. This gives us a better perspective and helps us to find solutions. It also gives us reassurance that we can manage day-to-day problems. When you look back through your journal entries of even a few days ago, you will see that you got through a difficult period and this will give you the courage to continue.

You can buy a special notebook you'll enjoy writing in but keep it somewhere safe as you don't want anyone else to be reading what you've written. It's for your eyes only.

I recommend writing in your journal all the way through the ten steps to beating depression. However, there is one type of writing technique I'll be referring to throughout the book that needs more of an introduction and explanation and that's non-dominant writing.

Non-dominant hand writing

The non-dominant hand writing activity is designed to help you access those parts of yourself you may have ignored for years. When we're depressed we are not in tune with the wise and sometimes vulnerable part we keep hidden inside. However, this wise and sensitive part of us is full of intelligence on how to make our lives better. As we get older we tend to push away these instincts and, in the process, we push away our creativity, which is fundamental to our well-being. We all have the answers to the challenges that face us and it's a case of reuniting with that hidden part of us when we're struggling with life's problems to help us get back on our feet.

Non-dominant hand writing is done with the hand you do not

write with. If you write with your right hand, your non-dominant hand is the left, and if you write with your left hand, your non-dominant hand is the right. Your non-dominant hand is connected to your intuition and emotion whereas your dominant hand is connected to your conscious, thinking side. Once you pick up a pen in your non-dominant hand you're automatically writing from a child-like standpoint. It's hard to get the words to look right and even holding the pen can feel awkward. However, the words you write are straight from the heart and can help you access your true feelings about something when you are unaware of these.

Once you begin writing with your non-dominant hand you may be surprised at the words falling on the page. You may become frightened at the strength of the feelings that are released because they've probably been buried for some time. But the amazing thing is that you can then use your dominant hand to support your more vulnerable self. This activity works best when you use two pages of your journal. So if you are right-handed you write with your left hand on the left-hand page of your journal and respond with your right hand on the right-hand page of the journal and vice versa if you're left-handed.

Here's a quick example:

Non-dominant hand	Dominant hand
I feel sad today.	Why do you feel sad?
Because I'm lonely.	You're not alone, it just feels like that.
But there's no one here.	Well, I'm here for you.
Yes, but only for now.	I'll be here every day from now on.
OK, promise?	Yes I promise.

As simplistic as this looks, it really works. While you explore yourself through non-dominant writing you may find that the language you use with the different hands seems to come from two separate parts of you. And it does! One is expressing feelings whilst the other is expressing logic. It helps to bring you closer to yourself and it works very quickly.

This activity is used in the ten steps to help you find things that you can focus on and help break through the fog of depression.

You may find that by doing this activity regularly your life may become simpler. What's exciting is how we recognize that our needs are actually very simple. We don't need to conquer the world; all we really want is to feel peaceful.

Meditation

The meditations in this book are designed to help you get back in touch with your creative inner resources, which are vital in helping beat depression fast. These resources get ignored when we're in the darkness and madness of depression. Yet these resources play a critical role in breaking the vicious cycle of depression through the emotion, mind and body connection. A mindful meditation has the power to pierce through depressive thoughts instantly and carry us back to what really brings us joy, appreciating the present moment.

There is a whole raft of research backing up the claims that mindfulness meditation can seriously dent depression but these findings are totally useless unless we actually feel the difference. The bottom line is that when we're depressed we're fixated on trying to *change our feelings* so we can escape the horribleness of the despair. However, the fastest way to beat depression is to *accept the depressive feelings* because this takes their negative power away. Once the acceptance has been acknowledged, the joy waits for us. This is how meditation can achieve real change.

Although meditation may sound like hard work it really isn't. When meditating it's helpful to sit or lie down (but then depression is probably making you feel tired anyway), you need to pause (but depression stops us all in our tracks) and you are asked simply to be aware of your breathing and listen to positive suggestions. The meditations in this book really won't take very much effort. The only work you have to do is to remember to practise them.

Which meditation is which?

The meditation in *Step 1: Acceptance* is the mainstay meditation. It's ten minutes long and if nothing else this is the meditation to do every day. By bringing this meditation into your daily routine you will begin to feel profound changes and liberation, usually within a few days. The meditations in the following steps are adaptations of the one in the first step. They are designed to provide multiple benefits for sufferers of depression by targeting the issues raised in each particular step.

Record them yourself

The best way to personalize these meditations is to read the scripts off the page and into a phone, PC or other recording device. Your own voice is the one your mind accepts the best. Make sure you're in a quiet, still frame of mind when you record them. In each of the meditation scripts there are dots to indicate a pause of approximately one second. Music is not necessary to accompany these meditations.

How often should I meditate?

I recommended you practise two meditations each day to beat depression fast, perhaps one in the morning and one in the evening. Each meditation is ten minutes long but if you wanted to meditate for longer, you can re-record the meditation inserting longer pauses to ensure you are getting the most fulfilling experience each time you settle down to meditate.

What if I can't?

The meditations are there to give you the time to be . . . well, you. Can you make the time to be yourself? It's hard to find the time to be you because you may be too busy trying not to be you! This is why you have to make the space available. This is 'the work' that helps us beat depression fast. If you can't make the time then you could sleep ten minutes less each night to practise the meditations; they are the foundation of your recovery from depression.

Where should I meditate?

It's important to feel comfortable, safe and undisturbed. Can you make the space to meditate where you won't be interrupted and you can relax? Being relaxed, comfortable, warm and safe will help you to focus on each meditation so that you can allow the power of each meditation to seep into your soul and nourish you from within.

You can lie down or sit down (except for the walking and eating meditations) – it's up to you. You can close your eyes or keep them open, whatever feels more comfortable. The idea is to be awake, but if you fall asleep, that's not a problem and what it tells you is that you have a sleep debt. Once you wake up, if you have time, return to the meditation.

A note on thoughts whilst meditating

One thing to note is that our minds want to travel. They love to be active and will play a huge part in this meditation. This is normal and the key is not to fight the mind. If you find thoughts are dominating you, try to be kind to yourself and not criticize yourself. No one starts meditating with a still mind. Everyone experiences lots of thoughts. Sometimes the thoughts are completely manic. This is normal. The way to manage them is simply to let them go – let them float away – like a cloud in the sky floating past you. Once you notice you are having thoughts, simply bring your attention back to your breath.

Acceptance happens when we accept our thoughts as part of the meditation. If we try to stop them then they become all-powerful and we won't feel the peace. If we allow the thoughts to be just as they are, we are no longer dominated by them.

Affirmations

At the end of each step are affirmations. These are simple and loving declarations of the truth. They are there for you to say to yourself or out loud. They are universal and applicable to everyone. Say them in the morning before you start your day.

Go at your own pace

In spite of this book having a linear path, like many self-help books, it doesn't *have to* be followed step by step. It's the sign of a good self-help book when you can leaf through the pages and randomly stop to read something that offers some pertinent guidance. I hope you are able to do this in *Beat Depression Fast*.

CHAPTER 4

An Invitation

Please join me on this journey. I know the struggle of depression and I understand the loneliness, hopelessness and helplessness. I hope you will find words in this book to help you. Having said that, I don't have all the answers, I only know what worked for me. And sharing my story with others has helped me reconnect to the rest of humanity. I can't make promises but I can hold out my hand and ask you to give these ideas a try. These are age-old ideas that have been brought into the 21st century and they are getting results. They really are working. Please don't give up before you're half-way through. If nothing else, stay with the daily meditation in *Step 1*.

No one said the road to recovery is easy. It's often called 'the road less travelled' and that's exactly what it is. Recovering from depression can bring us to painful realizations but in learning to accept them, letting go and finding new ways of taking care of ourselves we come to a totally new way of living which, in the end, far exceeds the life we lived before.

Whenever you remember, bring your attention into this present moment where there are no problems. If you think about just that – what problems are there in this moment? Right now? None! If there were you would be off solving them, not reading this sentence. That is the power of mindfulness.

Please stay in touch. I wish you an amazing journey.

PART TWO

The Ten Steps

Acceptance

The first step to freedom

Modern life can be very confusing for people who suffer from depression. On the one hand it seems that everyone else is having an amazing time – smashing goals, enjoying brilliant relationships, getting great jobs and living life to the max. On the other hand, those of us who suffer from depression know only too well what it feels like to be on the opposite side, living in the darkness. While everyone else is 'getting on with their lives' we've got our noses pressed up against that window, looking at other people being happy and wondering how the hell we got here and how are we going to get out?

Then again you may have given up hope that you will ever get out. If you're suffering from depression it may seem like the chance of ever living a 'normal' life again is simply a world away; so far, in fact, that you've given up the idea that it could ever happen to you. The drudgery, the hopelessness, the feelings of meaninglessness and nothingness may be all you know. It can really feel like a physical barrier separating you from the rest of the world.

You may have tried lots of alternatives to fight your way out of the dark room. You may have engaged in a plan that's going to help you *think your way out of it*. You may have taken the right medication in the hope this will automatically *change the way you feel* without having to do anything else. Some of you may have tried really hard to achieve goals like getting a perfect job, house, girlfriend, husband, outfit, etc., hoping then you would feel better. You've probably read a lot of stuff on the web, bought books and paid for spa days, positive-thinking seminars or even therapists, tried new interests, got a new job or forced yourself to be more sociable, all in the hope that something out there will take away the misery of depression.

Many of you may have also committed to high-risk behaviours to try and escape the inner torment – I know I did. In my case it was workaholism, but whether it's alcohol, drugs (recreational or prescription), extreme exercise, crime, bulimia, pornography fixation, food bingeing, chain smoking or anything else, it's generally the case that once the bender is over, you find yourself left with a bigger hole in your life than before. I found that not only did I still have to deal with my depression but I now also had a voice beating me up and telling me how useless and pathetic I was for engaging in this destructive behaviour.

In a bid to make sense of all of this, it's time to accept the unacceptable: that we can't magically make depression disappear any more than we can force the sun to start shining because we want it to. The feelings of depression come from a place deep inside us – and are there to protect us and make us function properly.

Excuse me? Did you say protect us?

Yes, I did. There is a very, very good reason why we suffer from depression and it's the deeper part of us that's brought us to this point.

We are in this black place for a reason even though that reason may not be apparent yet. At this moment can you hold the thought that you are in the right place at the right time? This may sound utterly defeatist, but being at the point of defeat is a starting point. Before we can find our way out of depression, the best course of action is to accept the defeat.

One sufferer wrote:

> I'm always beating myself up for not being where I could be by now if I had done this or that, not being

where people my age are at. Is it fair to say that's because all this time I've been suffering depression/anxiety at various levels and it was a part of my life just like any other thing would have been? I don't mean using it as an excuse, like to say it's not my fault, I was busy with depression then but I'm trying to find ways of living with myself, accepting myself and not hating myself as much.

Whilst trying to find ways of beating the depression this sufferer explained what I too discovered. By going over and over what I should do to try and pull myself out of the depression, I ended up simply diving deeper into it. There was no salvation in trying to work out the whys and hows at this first critical point. Those thoughts only drove me deeper into the abyss. I would wake up each morning *determined* not to be beaten down by depression that day only to discover by nightfall that nothing had worked. By not accepting the depression I moved further into the dark room. By accepting the depression I *took away all resistance to it.*

Moving away from resistance

Resisting depression creates an inner conflict. It's like the swinging of a pendulum. At one end of its swing you may be saying: 'I don't want to feel like this' and feeling angry and frustrated. At the other end of the swing you might be saying: 'I will never be able to conquer this', whilst feeling hopeless and defeated. This swinging from one side to the other is exhausting but doesn't help us in our search for peace. We want to feel something other than depression. We would give anything to feel peaceful.

The irony is that as long as we *fight* depression, we strengthen it and lose our way. But, by accepting it, step by step, we diminish the power it holds over us. If we can find the courage to accept the depression for what it is – a phase of our lives that we have to pay attention to – we will begin to create an opening that will help us to move towards the light. We release energy that we need to recover, energy that's taken up with non-acceptance of the depression; energy that we can now use to our advantage: to get us on the path of recovery from depression and towards hope.

You won't come to any harm

You may not be able to bear the thought of accepting your depression. Maybe you are thinking, doesn't that just take me deeper into the hole of darkness and hopelessness? No, you won't come to any harm. Instead you will start the healing because you will begin to value your self. You may fear that if you stop fighting you will lose all control. This doesn't happen. You will become stronger because you release the recovery energy you are currently using to fight depression.

Acceptance doesn't mean accepting everything – just the depression

When I accepted my depression I accepted that at this very moment I was unable to fight it any longer. Something happened inside me: a shift from believing I could change this moment to recognizing that this moment was the reality of my situation. People who become totally accepting of their depression are taking positive action. The positive action is: 'I don't judge myself for being in this place.' This is the starting point of healing which leads to profound change and a new life.

You don't have to accept all the negative things in your life, just the depression. This in itself may give you clarity because depression seems to make everything seem grey. Once you start to accept the depression, it seems to lose its hold. This is because, when we continually try to escape from depression, we identify with it and nothing else. But we are not just the depression. The depression is something that is present in our lives now but it is a *temporary state*. We don't have to accept that we will be depressed for ever and that there will be nothing else.

It might help to think about the advice experts give to a person who has fallen into quick sand. Don't struggle – you'll only sink deeper. Instead pause, take a breath, spread out your arms and balance yourself. Accepting we're in the quicksand is the first step towards getting out. With depression, acceptance is about moving away from 'the struggle' and finding new ways of releasing ourselves from the hold it has on us.

What if the depression is too awful to accept?

If you feel that the depression is too awful to accept, try this. Accept the depression as if you'd chosen it. Seeing it as something you have a choice over is a way of taking the sting out of the tail. You may think this is mad but it is 'radical acceptance'. Radical acceptance is the ultimate approach to letting go of resisting the reality. I know I'm asking you to go further towards the 'enemy' and you may not be certain this is the right way but it is the way to beat depression *fast*. When you radically accept the depression you stop it in its tracks because you are no longer creating more pain. The mind stops going over and over the past – because you accept it. The mind stops projecting into the future – because you accept it. When you slow down the mind (more of that later) you stop creating more and more pain.

Three ways this helps us to beat depression fast

The first reason that acceptance helps us to beat depression fast is because accepting the depression helps us to accept the reality of our situation and, ultimately, ourselves. In saying out loud 'I accept I'm depressed', we inadvertently accept that we cannot manage it any more or that we can't go on with the way things have been. We allow the relief of that knowledge to flood into us. Instead of using all our energy to hold it back, we're allowing the dam to burst.

Non-acceptance creates more pain and hopelessness. So, in totally accepting the depression, we allow ourselves the luxury of hitting our 'rock bottom'. When we hit 'rock bottom' we have no place else to go. When we accept, we feel in harmony with ourselves because we can start to accept ourselves as being imperfect and fallible. Yes, we may be at our lowest ebb but this is where the soul whispers its secrets and shows us the road to healing. There is nobility and grace about accepting the depression. Nobility and grace live within all of us and they are the purest form of humanity, which can serve to nourish us as we put aside our weapons against the depression.

The second reason that acceptance helps us heal is because we accept the past. If, like me, you've suffered from a deep, 'life-eating' depression you probably have a tendency to ruminate about what's happened in the past. Your head may be full of thoughts about trying to fix the past, regrets about how you handled situations, guilt about your past behaviour or shame about who you were. When you accept the depression you also accept that life hasn't always turned out how you wanted. Out of the acceptance comes serenity, true spirituality and salvation. You will become free of the past, no longer pulled back like you're on a bungee cord, free to move forward to your true horizon. You come to see acceptance as the only way forward.

The third reason that acceptance helps us recover from depression fast is because it takes away the fear. When you accept the fear, instead of running from it, you turn around and face it. Fear is like a taunting bully who cowers in the face of self-respect. Facing it fills you with hope and gives you the courage you need to pull towards the light. The deflectors – fear and denial – won't hold you back any more.

Acceptance may be all you need

If you do nothing else but accept the depression, it may be all you need to move towards healing. To feel acceptance is to let go of everything you've needed to hang on to in your past to try and stay afloat in today. Yes, this can seem a foolish strategy at first and one that may seem too hard. However, practise this one day at a time and if you allow yourself this gift – regardless of the shape it comes in – you will feel the reward: an inner space which frees you from the fighting.

Some practical suggestions on how to accept the depression

1. Put down the weapons that you use to fight the world. You know – those thoughts that go around in the head:

- No one understands what I'm going through.
- I'll never get through this.
- There's no point.
- No one can help me.
- This is stupid advice, it'll never work.

2. Let the idea of becoming a pacifist, instead of a warrior, flow through you and see how that feels.
3. If you can, take some time out. For example: stay in bed, relinquish unnecessary commitments, keep life to a minimum and try to delegate tasks.
4. Put away your social masks for now because now is the time to pay attention to you and your recovery, and you don't need the pressure of entertaining anyone else too.
5. Take a break from playing the hero. Many of us try to maintain the image that we are achievers. Yes, we have achieved many things but now is the time to achieve recovery from depression; make this your priority.
6. Slow down and allow the natural healing process to begin. As you give up the resistance you will need your energy to nourish yourself. Finally the time has come when you are ready to accept this depression, and to beat it fast you need time and space for you.
7. Here's one way to accept the depression moment to moment: A.L.L.

- A-ccept the depression at this moment.
- L-et go of trying to make this moment be any different.
- L-ook at what choices I can make now.

You start with *accepting* the feeling, sensation, fatigue or harmful thoughts. That might seem like an ironic place to start but hear me out. Life is a little more beautiful every time you're able to accept this moment as it is. You may need to take this on trust for the moment.

You then *let go* of trying to make this moment any different from what it is. Just let go of how you think it could be and accept it how it is. And, finally, when the rapid thoughts have subsided, a little space will emerge – just enough for you to gain a perspective and *look* at what choices you have.

For example, you've run for the bus and just missed it. Holy shit! Now what? You're going to miss your very important meeting. Ahhhg! You're so upset and then the depressive thinking steps in: *you're so useless, you can't do anything right, you can't even manage to get the bus!*

Step in **A.L.L.** Accept you've missed the bus . . . Let go of trying to make this present moment any different to how it is. Once the peace has returned, Look at what other choices you have to make the meeting or to get it postponed and ask: what can I do to solve this problem?

Acceptance isn't ignoring or resisting the depression and it's not forgetting you have it. At the same time, acceptance isn't about believing the depression or doing what it's telling you to do. Acceptance is about creating a space to let whatever is going on go on, without needing to change anything.

It takes courage to practise acceptance but the promise is: it can give you your life back.

Begin with accepting small things like your room being messy or losing a coin. Before you're onto the big things you'll be laughing about missing the bus. Laughing at the absurd things we get upset about puts them in perspective. It also opens you up to what is precious. It's hard to appreciate what good things you have when you are constantly struggling against everything. But once acceptance becomes an everyday part of your life, you will begin to see what you have, instead of what you've lost. The shutters will open and you will see the beauty waiting for you outside.

ACTIVITIES

Honesty and acceptance about the depression

Open your journal and take some time to study these questions and answer them as honestly and thoroughly as you can, safe in the knowledge that no one else will ever see your answers.

Write with compassion for the part of you that's felt lonely and is hurting. That's the voice that needs your attention and your help:

* How am I powerless over the depression?
* What does my depression look/feel like?
* What does my depression give me?
* And am I ready to let that go?
* What does acceptance mean to me?
* What will I lose by accepting the depression?
* Conversely, what will I gain if I accept the depression?
* How has the depression looked after me?

What do I need to accept?

There are many things that prevent us from accepting the reality of this moment. This activity helps to determine what they are:

* What thoughts or memories or feelings am I trying to avoid?
* How do I avoid them, or, alternatively, what do I do to keep them away?
* What does this cost me?
* Who else suffers when I try to avoid thoughts, memories or feelings?
* How do I hurt myself when I try to avoid thoughts, memories or feelings?

By responding to these questions you will gain insight into your relationship with depression, how it's helped you or hindered you, and how you avoid it. This isn't an opportunity to self-criticize but a moment to get to know yourself a little bit better.

Mindfulness meditation for acceptance

This meditation is the main meditation to help beat depression fast. It's designed to last about ten minutes. It can be read through and followed from the text but it's best to use your own voice as a guide. So, if possible, record into a phone, tablet, PC or other device. Remember that the dots equal a pause.

Get yourself into a comfortable position lying down on a bed or a blanket. Make sure you are undisturbed and warm. If you prefer to sit up then make sure you are sitting on a chair with a back that can support you and with your feet firmly on the floor. If you practise yoga and you want to sit in the lotus position that is also fine as long as you can support your back.

Close your eyes and take a large breath in and slowly let it out . . . . breathe in again and slowly let it out . . . . out which will instantly decrease stress levels.

Now bring your awareness to your body . . . . and get a sense of where your body is lying or sitting on the bed or chair. Allow yourself to explore the places where physical contact is made with your body. Feel a connection to the solid structures that you are sitting or lying on . . . . And now focus your attention on your feet as if two pairs of hands are touching your feet on either side. Feel the sensations and the warmth on your feet while these invisible hands are caressing them . . . . Feel every part of your feet as the warmth from the hands caresses your soles and your toes and the tops of your feet and the heels and ankles . . . . Now bring your attention up to your calves and become aware of the hands caressing each calf . . . . Now bring your awareness to the shins and feel the hands caressing these parts of your legs . . . . Now bring your attention to your knees and thighs and imagine the two pairs of hands holding the tops of your legs and feel the warmth flooding through this part of your body . . . . And bring your awareness now to your abdomen and feel the hands being placed on either side of your abdomen and feel the warmth flooding through you . . . . And now bring your attention to your chest area and feel the two pairs of hands holding your chest area one in the front and one in the back and become aware of the physical sensations in your chest and around it as the warmth travels through your body . . . . And now feel the sensations as hands move up to your shoulders and you feel a pair of hands warming each shoulder . . . . And now feel the sensation of the hands going down your left arm all the way to the fingertips.... And now the hands are moving down your right arm warming it up as they move down to the fingertips.... And now feel the physical sensation of both sets of hands moving from your neck up to the top of your head and encasing the whole of your head with warmth as they caress it.

Now bring your attention to your breath.... And notice the pattern of your breath as it moves in through the nose, down into the abdomen, then back up and out through the nose.... Just be aware of the physical sensations that take place while you become aware of your breath.... As you stay with your breath your mind may wander on a thought but just let the thought disappear like a cloud moving along the sky.... And gently bring your attention back to your breath and become aware of your breath going into the abdomen and out through your nose.... Observe each breath at a time.... You can notice that right in this moment you can accept the way it is.... And as thoughts return be kind to them and let them go and bring your attention back to your breath.... Knowing that right at this moment everything is the way it's meant to be.... Your body, your breath, your thoughts are all as they are meant to be.... And allow yourself to accept this moment and to surrender to this moment.... Allowing the breath to be just as it is.

Following this meditation twice a day for one week will begin your recovery from depression. It certainly takes a leap of faith to get started but the results will be quite extraordinary.

AFFIRMATIONS

I accept every part of me including the depression which lives inside me. I no longer have to struggle with the blackness; today I can accept it and it won't overwhelm me.

I'm not a depressed person but I sometimes experience depression. I have many sources of strength to help me recover from the depression. The way out of this depression will become obvious to me, and it won't be long.

Today I can accept that I am a fallible human being with all my imperfections. I can now see that being whole means being incomplete. I no longer need to blame myself for feeling depressed or beat myself up or practise self-hate.

Today I can let go of needing to control everything in my life and surrender to the 'higher good' that awaits me.

Trust

Letting a greater power into your life

"Trust? You have got to be kidding! Trust who? Who in their right mind trusts anyone? Or anything?"

When we are dealing with the despair and hopelessness of depression, it's almost impossible to believe that everything's going to turn out OK. Right now, it doesn't feel OK to feel this depressed. Depression and self-belief do not go together. You may be too angry to trust in anything or anyone. You may think, if there was anything out there that could help me then I wouldn't be in this space I'm in now!

In the dark rooms of depression trusting that something or someone else can help us is a tall order. Many of us have set ourselves up as the 'something else' or the 'all-knowing one', believing that nothing out there can help us. We have shunned others' help because we think they don't understand how we feel. We feel so ashamed at how needy we are that we can't allow anyone else to see that part of us. We've tried to keep others away by ignoring offers of help. Or we've felt so desperate that we've literally been hanging on to their ankles as they're trying to get out the door. The thoughts go round and round trying to make sense of the depression. This isolation taps into the mindset that if we try harder, be nicer, ignore our fear, zip up our emotions, beat up that small part of us that's hurting and get on with it, then we can recover from depression. But it doesn't work.

For me, real change didn't happen until I acknowledged that I couldn't beat depression on my own and that I needed to rely on something bigger and wiser than myself. I realized it was pure arrogance on my part to believe I was the most powerful thing in life and that there was nothing more powerful. This step came as a blessed relief as I recognized I could step back and let something else take up the slack.

This thing which is bigger and more powerful than me is very real. I like to call it my higher power but there are other terms you might prefer – the kingdom of heaven, fate, the future, instinct, God, a collective conscience of a group of people or even a total human collective awareness. Whatever its title I have found a very real force beyond my conscious mind that has helped me beat depression.

There may be some of you saying, 'Oh yes, hang on a minute – really? I don't think so! I'll believe it when I see it.' This reaction is totally understandable so let me try to explain further. Our higher power will help us to accept the support we badly need from a deeper source or a power greater than our conscious self. Our conscious self is the part of us we know well – the part of us that thinks our way through life. But our higher power is a bigger, wiser part of us, beyond the daily worrying and anxiety of the conscious mind. Through meditation you can help connect to this still space that is calm and serene. Once you've experienced that calmness you will find that the worries or thoughts that seemed so distressing diminish and you will create new solutions to problems that perplexed you. Through the regular practice of mindfulness and acceptance you can continue to deepen your connection to your higher power. Once you've taken some small steps and gained some confidence you will see it's always been there for you.

It's not religion

It's not so much that we have to believe in a power greater than us. It's that we come to realize that our over-thinking mind is not the highest power there is. This isn't about religion, it's about spirituality. I believe there is a life spirit that we can learn to trust in – and it's accessible at the still centre we can find when we meditate.

Depression is a spiritual dilemma, not a religious deficiency. As our minds become clearer we need to release the grip of our conscious control and allow our true spirit to emerge. We can learn to reconnect with that hidden part of us, the part that we can turn to knowing that the future will be OK. As our trust in that powerful part of ourselves grows, we learn to lean into the flow of the river rather than swim against it. We can beat depression faster if we let ourselves recognize this higher power.

For some of you, this suggestion might feel frustrating. You may have felt angry with a power greater than you for abandoning you in times of trouble. This is especially true for people who have assigned a list of negative traits to a greater power, such as punishment, shame and guilt. You might think of a greater power as something that you were told to respect and pray to when you were a child but who then disappeared just when you needed help most. You may be angry, with feelings of rejection and desertion. And I know it's hard to see how you can reclaim any faith in there being anything that you can't see or touch being able to help you.

There is a fable about God helping someone in trouble:
A man is on top of a roof during a great flood. Someone comes by in a boat and says 'Get in, get in!' The man on the roof replies, 'No I have faith in God, he will grant me a miracle.'

Later, when the water is up to his waist, another boat comes by and the sailor tells him to get in. The man on the roof responds that he has faith in God and God will give him a miracle. With the water at about chest high, a third boat comes to rescue him, but the man turns down the offer again saying that God will grant him a miracle.

With the water at chin height, a helicopter arrives, the crew throw down a ladder and they tell him to get in. Mumbling, with the water in his mouth, he again turns down the request because of his faith in God.

He arrives at the gates of heaven with broken faith and says to St Peter, 'I thought God would grant me a miracle and I have been let down.' Peter chuckles and responds, 'I don't know what you're complaining about; we sent you three boats and a helicopter.'

Sometimes we can only see in hindsight the help that was available to us and we can miss what we have right at this moment. We don't have to be religious or God-fearing to understand that there is a 'God-like' part of us that knows what is right for us and can point us in the right direction.

Let's look at some of the attitudes and behaviours you can begin to explore that can help bring you closer to your inner higher power.

Willingness

Let's start with willingness. Willingness is the opening of the heart to be present and available in your life and accept the changes that are an inevitable part of the journey. Willingness isn't effort – it's being in a state of effortlessness. It's accepting what we must accept to recover from depression. Being willing to be open to the journey is the next step on from acceptance – the step we looked at in the previous chapter. Like opening the door to some dinner guests and welcoming them into your home, regardless of whether you like them or not, willingness is an acknowledgement that you should walk this path no matter who or what turns up.

In practical terms, willingness is letting go of control. Being willing is scary because we're in the unknown. We're not sure how to let go of controlling everything around us to keep ourselves safe. But let's look at this more closely. True willingness is letting go of what you've relied on up until now, and I'm guessing it hasn't been working for you. Perhaps now is the time to try a different approach.

Here's another story that illustrates how we can hang on to old ways of behaving:

The tiger, the man, the god

A man was being chased by a tiger. He ran as hard as he could until he was at the edge of a cliff with the tiger in hot pursuit. The man looked over the edge of the cliff and saw a branch growing out of the side of the cliff a few feet down. He jumped down and reached the branch just as the tiger reached the edge of the cliff. The tiger growled viciously as the man sighed a great sigh of relief.

Just then, a mouse came out from a crevice and began to chew on the branch. The man looked down to the drop of a thousand feet and sure death and looked to the heavens and yelled out, 'Oh God, if you are there, please help me. I will do anything you ask but please help!'

Suddenly a voice came booming down from heaven, 'You will do anything I ask?' it questioned.

Shocked to hear a reply to his question, the man yelled back, 'I will gladly do anything you ask, but please save me!'

The voice from heaven then replied, 'There is one way you can be saved but it will take courage and faith.'

The branch began to weaken from the mouse's efforts and the tiger was still growling a few feet above, 'Please, Lord, tell me what I must do and I will do it. Your will is my will.'

The voice from heaven said, 'Let go of the branch.'

The man looked down to a fall of a thousand feet and certain death. He saw the mouse still chewing on the branch and the hungry tiger a few feet away. Then he looked up at the heavens and screamed, 'Is there anyone else up there?'

Like the man in the fable, when we are depressed we hold on to the branch for dear life, unwilling to let go but begging for help. What kind of branch are you hanging on to? Perhaps it's another person whom you are unwilling to let go because you're scared of being alone. Perhaps you are hanging on to a lifestyle that you can no longer afford because you are frightened what others might say. We hold on to what is familiar for fear of facing change. We are frightened that if we let go we will 'lose it' altogether by falling into the abyss. This is a common anxiety for those of us who have suffered from depression, and I know it's very frightening.

But what are the options if we don't try something different? I know that for a long time I depended on my self-reliance to protect me. I had been taught to be self-sufficient at any cost and to trust that I was the only person who could help me. But, the downside was that I felt lonely, resentful and hopeless. I may have appeared confident but I was often aloof or secretive, keeping others away because it was too painful to let anyone know how I really felt. I struggled in relationships or needed to rely on medication to lessen the pain.

It was when my back was against the wall that I was most open to change. Putting in place the idea that I could rely on something other than my desperately controlling conscious mind helped to free me from the burden of depression. Reaching out, in the belief that something other than my self-control could help me, enabled me to feel liberated.

Keeping an open mind

Try to keep an open mind to the possibility that connecting with this higher power can restore you to a sense of peace. Depression affects our minds, bodies and spirit. This is the point where we heal our spirit by taking the step towards a greater, loving power. We start by asking for courage to help us become whole again and to help us pick up the pieces of our shattered selves. This work doesn't come easy and we must take tiny steps. We will fall down many, many times but that doesn't mean we won't recover. Like a small child who takes their first steps and falls over, we will gradually build the confidence we need to believe that we are OK and that everything will turn out OK.

Our real parent

Although our mothers gave birth to us, our true parent is our higher power. Our life's journey is to learn to reconnect with this power and discover our real selves by letting go of the legacy left by our parents. We walk away from the mould our parents made for us and reconnect to this loving force that can help us to re-frame our past and look towards a radiant future. When we look back we will see that the depression we suffered has been a supreme asset.

How to contact our higher power

We all have our own way of speaking to that deep soulful part of us that is connected to our higher power. It may be that you find the support with a prayer. It may be that you make the connection by writing out your deepest feelings in a journal and asking your higher power to help you. Explore what works best for you.

When I feel desperate and I can't think of what else to do I just ask my higher power to take over. I see myself in the driving seat of a car and then I climb into the back seat and ask my higher power to take over. In my mind's eye I imagine myself looking at the back of His head with His hands on the steering wheel driving the car and I instantly feel my stress melt. I have to remember to do this but when I do, it works! *Wendy*

When my life is in a mess I know it's because I've tried to run everything myself. So now when I find myself running around in circles I stop and ask God to help me by putting my finger on my chest and asking it – him – whatever – to take over. It's just a way I tell myself, 'Time to drop the control'. Sometimes I have to do it every five minutes. I go 'Oh Christ what am I going to do?' then I remember, put my finger on my chest and it makes me think 'I don't have to do anything because I can ask God to take over.' If I do this when things are really bad, within an hour it feels different and I feel better. *Marcus*

So – what I did to try and believe in a higher power was – I tried. I tried super hard. I begged for help by getting on my knees and praying, praying, praying. I did this all day long. I tried to do what I'd heard was the way to experiment with prayer – you know, to try it out to see if it worked in my life so that each time I prayed and had a positive experience related to that prayer, it's like I was gathering evidence in a scientific experiment. And it's through that process that I was able to come to believe in something greater than myself. Because praying does work. Or, at least, it did for me. It made me feel better. It made me feel grounded and hopeful. It helped me to feel connected. And, I'd say more than anything else, it just helped to distract me. I mean, prayer thoughts help me replace the thoughts I'd normally be having – you know, thoughts about what a piece of shit I was and how much I'd fucked up my life. So prayer definitely gave me relief. *Jay*

How believing in a higher power helps us beat depression *fast*

Essentially, developing trust is about *letting go* of trying to control everything outside of us and learning to rely on our higher power. Our need to control could be one reason why we've ended up in the dead-end alley of depression. Needing to feel *certain* about what goes on around us curtails our own natural resilience. We don't trust our own calm and wise inner voice and, having silenced it maybe for years, we can't hear it any more. Yet that voice longs to be heard and it's waiting for us to listen.

Our higher power is the highest level inside us, connected to our higher Self, our core existence. It's not outside us or separate from us. Once we accept this and begin to connect with it, we will start to experience the limitless power and intelligence that life has to offer. It's as if the universe is living inside us, and meditation is the way to experience this power. This is the 'work' that helps us develop trust that, not only will everything be OK, but essentially, we are OK, right now.

By undertaking the activities and listening to the meditation, for one week, we can begin to reconnect with the part of us that holds our intuition, the 'god' part of us. This is where our true voice lives and it's this voice that we can turn to in times of turmoil for the answers we mistakenly believe are to be found outside of us. This meditation facilitates a two-way communication between us and our wise self. By repeating these activities and coming to rely on this higher power, our willingness to trust will grow. We develop insight, knowledge and faith and we often find answers within minutes.

Sometimes it's as simple as a prayer

Here is an example of a morning prayer and an evening prayer:

Morning:
God, take my life into your hands;
Show me your plan for me today;
And give me the power to carry it out.

Evening:
Higher power, grant me the serenity
To accept the things I cannot change,
The courage to change the things I can
And the wisdom to know the difference.

ACTIVITIES

Open your journal and use your *non-dominant* hand to answer the following questions fully; examples of brief answers are there to guide you to your own answers:

1. How have I tried to beat this depression through my own efforts?
   I have tried to force myself to be happier by ignoring my own feelings.
2. What have the results been of my own efforts?
   I've been more and more depressed and nothing has helped me get better.
3. What do I do on a daily basis that stops me from accepting that there may be a higher power who could help me?
   Get angry with everyone around me or feel victimized by them.
4. How does it feel to believe that there is nothing bigger than me who can help me beat this depression?
   Very lonely, lost and hopeless.

Now use your *dominant* hand to answer the following questions:

1. What does it feel like to accept completely that there may be something bigger to help me find the peace I crave?
   It feels like a relief because I've been trying on my own for a long time and it hasn't worked.
2. What do I need to be able to feel there is hope for me?
   I need to know that everything is going to be OK in the end and I need proof of that.
3. Can I believe that recovery from depression is also a spiritual journey? Describe what I think that journey will involve.
   I think it will involve me stopping hating myself so much and learning to like myself more.
4. How can I consider facing my own depression with the help of a higher power?
   I can only consider facing the depression if I know there is someone or something I can turn to in my darkest hour.

5. What do I need from a higher power to help me on that journey?
   I need to feel that a higher power is there.
6. How can I ask for that help on a daily basis?
   I can meditate to ask for help, or pray, or write down what I want in my journal.
7. How will I know I've received the help I need?
   When I feel better, less lonely and more hopeful.

Meditation to meet your higher power

Ideally, record this meditation with your own voice. Remember the dots mean a pause. Then, find 15 minutes to let it take you on a journey to your higher power:

Sit or lie down in a comfortable, safe place . . . . Make sure you can lie back and relax . . . . Now simply breathe in and out and let yourself sink into your chair or bed . . . . Thoughts will come into your mind . . . . do not fret, simply let them float away as quietly as they arrived . . . . just let them go . . . . do not hold on to them . . . . Notice your breath coming in and out of your body . . . . be aware of it travelling through your nose or mouth . . . . take a deep breath and hold it . . . . hold it . . . . hold it more . . . . keep holding it . . . . and let it go! . . . . and as it goes feel your body completely relax . . . . Notice the worry lines in your forehead relax and soften . . . . see how your jaw line loosens and your cheek muscles just drop . . . . feel your throat relax and let the tension out of your chest cavity . . . . feel the muscles of your stomach drop and relax . . . . feel the whole weight of your body sink into your chair . . . . You have no worries or cares right now . . . . let them drift away with your thoughts . . . . you are in a lush, green forest . . . . smell the forest smell and see the damp green blanket of grass sprinkled with sunbeams . . . . You are on the edge of a river . . . . this river is beautiful . . . . it is long and wide and as still as a mirror . . . . there is a boat by the side of the river . . . . step into this boat . . . . it has big, sumptuous pillows for you to sink into . . . . make yourself comfortable . . . . You hardly have time to settle and the boat starts to move very gently . . . . it is gliding along like a gentle swan . . . . it is being guided and you have nothing to fear . . . . just sit back and enjoy the beauty of your surroundings . . . . don't worry if you cannot see them, just get a sense of being there . . . . all you can hear is the gentleness of trickling water as your boat moves along the flat river . . . . Sit back and relax and feel the moment with no cares and no worries . . . . in the distance you can see land . . . . there is a beautiful island ahead of you . . . . the boat is heading towards the island . . . . it feels very peaceful and the nearer you get to the island, the more peaceful you feel . . . . You reach the island and step out of the boat . . . . there is a mist over the island . . . . it feels very safe . . . . it is the most beautiful place you have ever seen . . . . you are mesmerized by the beauty of the forest, the sound of water, the humming of the trees . . . . You feel safer than you have ever felt before . . . . you breathe in the crisp air and let yourself relax, down . . . . down . . . . down . . . . down into the safety of this island . . . . you see a light in the distance . . . . the light is tiny and just shines through the mist . . . . you can see it moving towards you . . . . As it gets closer, you can feel the energy coming from the light . . . . you can feel a beauty inside you . . . . the light is getting brighter now and is much larger . . . . as the light gets closer, it's growing and growing and the energy you can feel from this light is like the love you have always longed for . . . . This feeling is filling you up and the circle of light is now the same size as you . . . . the brightness is beautiful and the beauty is filling every part of your body . . . . the light is right before you . . . . There are messages coming to you from the light . . . . 'You are a beautiful person and I love you more than life itself'.... 'I will always love you and protect you'.... your higher power's love fills you up even more.... Walk towards the light and step into the light until it surrounds you.... let the warmth and love fill you up even more.... relax your stomach muscles to allow the love into every part of you.... drink the love and let everything else go.... nothing else matters right now.... fall into the arms of this love and light.... Speak to your higher power and have a conversation with your higher power.... [take some time for this].... Now, step back from the light and let the love stay with you.... now your higher power has a message for you.... hold your hands out and allow your higher power to give you a ball of light.... take this light into your hands.... There is a message on the ball.... read it and when you have finished, gently let the ball go upwards and float away.... it is time to leave this island.... step into the boat and let it guide you back to the forest.... Know that you can come back to meet your higher power at any time you want.

AFFIRMATIONS

I can reach out to my higher power in the knowledge that is my true parent.

I turn my life over to my higher power and ask for healing. I know the only real security is being connected to my higher power.

I let the positive forces of my higher power work in my life. I can ask my higher power to be there for me no matter what. I accept my higher power's unconditional love for me.

My higher power shows itself to me as I am guided through the day. I can handle whatever life throws at me today because my higher power doesn't give me anything I can't cope with.

If I need help all I have to do is to hand over to my higher power and ask for the answers. I know the answers will come back to me at the right time.

Touching the Void

And awakening the heart

Anyone who has experienced a deep depression – a depression that's lasted weeks, months or maybe years – knows the darkness. The darkness of depression is like the darkness of a thick, black cloud. It settles on the soul like a concrete coat. It feels like a physical garment because it's tangible and touchable. When it has settled in, it's hard to see ahead. The darkness makes our eyes go foggy and our brains go cloudy. All we sense is a void inside us; a dark, bottomless void.

But there is another side to depression. This depression fog is a way of helping you to slow down and become more still. It helps you to give up what's not been working for you. It gives you the opportunity to transform your life and create positive change. It helps you catch up with yourself by slowing you down. Have you ever been pole-axed with fatigue – deep, deep fatigue that rendered you almost incapable of doing anything except the bare minimum to keep yourself alive? There's a reason for this.

Depression happens when we avoid our distressing emotions. It's brilliant. Most of us have buried emotions that would be very painful if we allowed them to surface. As we don't want to go through this experience, we unknowingly numb ourselves out – with depression. It's a fail-safe process that's there to keep us functioning in spite of having deep and painful emotions. However, our positive emotions also get thrown in the mix which means that when we suffer from depression, not only do we not feel our pain; we also *don't feel our joy.*

Research by Steven Hayes and others published in 2004 in *The Psychological Record* shows that when we can't feel our distressing emotions, we can't take proper care of ourselves. This is because we use numbing tactics to avoid feelings and these tactics are usually not good for us. We may resort to drinking, taking prescription or street drugs, or become extremely busy. However, when we become willing to experience and accept our distressing emotions, the same research shows that we can halve the severity of the depressive symptoms. In a nutshell, we can recover from depression, faster, if we allow ourselves to feel the negative emotions that the depression is so valiantly trying to press down.

Our culture *fanatically* promotes the idea of avoiding any emotion that might cause distress. If we succumbed to sadness or anxiety as a child we might well have been told to 'pull our socks up' and improve the way we behaved. We learned to grit our teeth and become a 'more productive human being' by burying our deeper feelings. As children we generally were never questioned if there was something wrong at a deeper level and we probably didn't have the vocabulary or the confidence to stand up to the authority figures in our lives. Depression can arise when we aren't allowed to express our negative emotions in a way that can truly be heard and understood.

In dealing with the outside world the culture we encounter is often based on the concept, 'if you don't like it, don't do it' or 'get rid of it'. In the short term this might help us get through the day but on a longer-term basis, this approach can stifle the person trapped inside. People who suffer deep depression are often very sensitive and may find that burying how they really feel about things is the only way to survive. But there is a price to pay.

Perhaps the following exchange sounds familiar to you.

You meet someone and their first greeting is: 'How are you?' And you reply: 'Fine thanks, how are you?' And they reply – 'I'm fine thanks.' **Fine** can also be defined as:

- F-rightened
- I-nsecure
- N-ervous
- E-motional

The words might sum up how you feel when you're meeting people you're not comfortable with.

Because we've learned and practised this behaviour for a long time, maybe for ever, it's deeply ingrained. We inadvertently feed this behaviour and, as we feed it, it grows bigger. The more we avoid our distress, the more it grows and the more frightening it becomes. The feelings of distress can become so frightening that our tactics to avoid them have to become big enough to overcome the fear.

If this is what you have been doing please don't beat yourself up over it. This is a perfectly logical response to a difficult set of circumstances – and you've been taught to respond in this way. You wouldn't have chosen to bury your feelings but that's the mould that was set up for you. Now, however, we are adults and it's up to us to change our responses to our own distress so we can feel better and beat the depression as fast as possible.

Stage one is to try to stop blaming yourself for feeling so defeated by depression. You didn't ask for it, you didn't invite it, and you didn't cause it. You've tried to deal with your pain and so far your methods may not seem to have worked but that doesn't mean you can't feel compassionate towards yourself for trying.

Now you're ready to try a different approach.

Willingness to let the distress out

As we saw in the previous chapter, *Step 2, Trust,* willingness is the opposite of control. In that step we looked at being willing to acknowledge a higher power within you. Now I want you to become willing to allow your emotions to break through the blanket of depression and come to the surface. I want you to adopt a loving approach to your hurting self as that will help you to feel safer. The emotions are buried because it doesn't feel OK for them to come out. But, if you nurture them, they will be released and this will unburden you. The goal here is not to feel happy but to feel more at peace – and that is a lasting benefit.

The path to freedom can sometimes take us in a direction we didn't want to go. There's a quote by a Buddhist nun called Pema Chodron about this journey. She says: 'In the process of discovering our true nature, the journey goes down, not up, as if the mountain pointed toward the earth instead of the sky. We move down and down and down, and with us move millions of others, our companions in awakening . . . right there we discover a love that will not die.' We can expand awareness and consecrate this journey, which will bring us hope that we can transform ourselves.

Discovering our emotional landscape

Think of yourself as a beautiful lake – majestic and alive. In the very depths of the lake lies your inner peace, the source of your lifeblood. The surface represents your conscious thinking mind. If the surface is turbulent, you will feel unsettled, if it's still, you will be at peace. In between the peaceful bottom and the surface lies your emotional landscape. The currents just beneath the surface swirl and tug, and consequently agitate your feelings. These currents use up precious resources because we pay so much attention to the emotions that are floating just below the surface. The chronic emotional turmoil acts as a barrier to the peace and stillness resting in the depths of the lake. If you release the emotional energy that has built up it will allow you access to the sacred tranquillity sitting there waiting for you. You can do this by identifying and releasing hidden feelings. But it is important to remember that *you are not your feelings*. Your feelings are a response to something that's happened. We all feel things all the time and we may have several feelings at once. But holding on to unacknowledged feelings can keep us trapped. Releasing them and accepting them can allow new responses and a lifting of the weight of past unhappiness.

Before we do this we need to begin by distinguishing feelings. If you have been depressed for many weeks, months or even years, you may not understand what feelings are. Depression may have taught you to *not* be in tune with your feelings. You may feel confused about what you feel. Naming feelings is an anathema and can make you feel frightened and want to run away. I know for me when I was in the midst of depression even the word 'feelings' could fill me with dread. Oddly enough I was excellent at identifying other people's feelings. In fact I sometimes based how I felt on what other people were feeling. In this way, by experiencing their moods, I felt safe and in control.

To be asked to 'release hidden feelings' can be tantamount to torture. But this work must be done if we want to recovery from depression – fast. There is no shortcut but once you get started, they'll be no stopping you. It's not easy – but then neither is being numbed out!

Let's not kid ourselves, however, this part is difficult. Avoiding our feelings is called 'numbing out' and is a common response to painful and distressing situations. But over time this can become a destructive way to live. It's a bit like driving a car with a clunky noise coming from the engine. We try turning up the radio to block the noise but that isn't dealing with the real issue. Even if we can't hear the engine noise any longer, we know it's still there. It's one more thing that will create more anxiety – anxiety that's already running high!

When you begin the practice of tuning back into your feelings, there may be a lag time where you're unsure of what you're feeling. This is because you may not be used to being in touch with them. But give yourself time and space. It may be helpful to think of feelings in the way Buddhists do – they describe them as 'clouds that pass by' and that is a very good description. Your feelings may be powerful but they will pass and new feelings will replace them.

By accepting powerful feelings you will find that they no longer have such power. If we think we have to suffer, the very thought tends to makes us suffer more. But, if we accept our suffering we can move beyond it. It is important to be gentle while you reconnect with that hidden part of yourself and take it a day at a time, an hour at a time, a minute at a time.

Let's get started

Here's a quick exercise you can do when you feel overwhelmed with powerful feelings. Fill in the blank spaces in any way you like.

> I am feeling _____. It is OK, I can allow myself to have this feeling. I can make space for it.... I don't have to be afraid of it, to try to get rid of it or to be caught up in it.
>
> I feel this emotion physically in my body in my _____. Breathe into this spot or spots one by one, three deep breaths in, three deep breaths out for each spot.
>
> _____ is just an emotion, just a feeling to be felt, nothing more and nothing less. *I am not my emotion.* I am an observer of my emotion.
>
> _____ is just like an ocean wave. It comes and it goes.... I can turn my attention to the present, noting my breathing, noticing what I see, hear, smell, and taste all around me.

Healing the feelings and finding the buried treasure

The promise of this book is that when you begin to acknowledge and respect the spectrum of feelings you have deep inside you, you will be able to release them and find the buried treasure of peace and tranquillity that lies beneath.

Levels of feeling awareness

When you first become aware of your feelings you may simply see them as good or bad, positive or negative. This is because we tend to be unaware of the full spectrum of our feelings. Generally speaking we have four different levels of awareness about our feelings.

- **The first level** is when we don't really feel our feelings. An example of this would be when someone asks you how you are and you actually don't know. You may report that you are 'fine', as that seems to be what people expect to hear, but in all honesty you couldn't actually describe how you feel.

- **The second level** is when we begin to explore our feelings. Once you realize you do have feelings then you become more aware of changes in your inner world but may still be confused as to what that means. You may tend to keep that information to yourself.

- **The third level** is when we begin to experience the feelings and we start to recognize them rather than simply feeling numbed out. This level can be quite scary if you've never really experienced your feelings. It can make you feel a bit out of control but it's important to recognize that these are just feelings; like clouds in the sky, they will pass.

- **The fourth level** of feeling awareness is when we begin to share our feelings with another person. You may stumble at this point because you're not really sure who to talk to or what to say.

Who to share with

In order to check who is safe to share your feelings with you can start by sharing just a little of your feelings with someone and then check the response. If you feel heard and not judged, and they support you, you may go back to them. Someone who doesn't try to jump in and fix you when you share your feelings is a good indicator of someone who might be able to *really listen* to you. A counsellor or a therapist is a brilliant person with whom to check out your feelings as you should feel safe and supported. However, there are many self-help groups that can also be a place to go to, for instance the various 12-step groups. You will find other suggestions in *How to Get Help* at the end of the book.

Once you begin to trust yourself and others with your feelings, amazing things begin to happen. One word from someone else can make the difference between feeling totally isolated and feeling completely at peace or 'normal'! It can bring a great sense of freedom and hope in knowing you're not alone. This is the beginning of a spiritual transformation.

The risks of sharing your feelings

Sharing your feelings is risky. But it's worth the risk because the rewards are magnificent. Sharing with others brings you on an equal level with people. You no longer have to depend on their approval or manipulate them for their attention. You may have been hiding your feelings from other people for fear of being judged. Now you know you can come out of the darkness and into the light and experience all of your feelings truthfully and share them honestly.

If you feel you need help in feeling comfortable trusting the people you want to share your feelings with, you may like to spend a little time meditating on the question, tuning into your still centre and checking your feelings from a place of calmness. The inner place of peace and calmness, the place I call your higher power, can be a very helpful guide here.

The next challenge you are likely to face is accepting loving support and praise from people with whom you have shared your feelings. We have a praise deficiency. We tend to dismiss praise because we've operated with shut down feelings. It is important to begin by praising ourselves first and that will lead us to accepting it from others. We can ask ourselves why we push others away. Once we can see that's how we behave, we can accept it. Once we accept it, things will change and we will learn to let others in.

Transforming our feelings to beat depression fast

It could be said that depression is a result of one feeling after another being ignored. Had we known that, we probably wouldn't have ignored them in the first place. But now we have some steps to move on and we can allow ourselves to become excited and hopeful.

The promise is:

> as we become aware of our painful feelings, we can then set them free. As each painful feeling is set free, we lift the burden on ourselves. As a result we will experience gratitude that we have discovered how to transform our pain into joy.

It's like a concert with the peaks and troughs, the high notes and the low notes, all working in harmony with our lives. There is no point in trying to ignore our feelings any longer. Our feelings are a vital part of our complete selves and we honour and respect ourselves when we do this feeling work.

The beauty of healthy pain

There is value in freeing ourselves from pain. This is the healthy road to recovery from depression. You may have experienced much pain in your life: heartbreak, despair, abuse, hopelessness and misery. But healthy pain is different. Healthy pain is healing and tears are the coins of the healing. It's a different feeling and comes from saying goodbye to the ways we've treated ourselves and others in the past. It's a soft pain that brings freedom and acceptance.

I know that when I was unwilling to acknowledge my hurt and suffered in silence I prolonged the agony. I dreaded having to open up to the pain because I was scared that, if I started to cry, I would never stop. But by acknowledging my hurt I finally brought depression to an end.

If you are feeling scared about opening out to your feelings, try turning to your higher power for guidance. In the still space of quiet prayer or meditation you will be heard. As I opened to my pain I found I never experienced more pain than I could handle. I found, for example, that it's almost impossible to cry for more than 15 minutes because the body has only got that many tears. After that it's dry heaving! Within an hour I felt the difference – lightness in the heart, a little less burden in the soul and a feeling of hope for recovery.

The tears that come at this time are the greatest healer.

A special note on anger

We need to pay careful attention to our anger because it's widely known that depression is anger turned inward. Suppressing anger is self-destructive because the negative energy redirects into the body. Anger is a fiery emotion whose purpose is to help us resolve problems, deep issues and internal conflict. It's like a pressure-release valve and it's better to release anger than to turn it inside and let it destroy us. However, we are *not taught* that it's healthy to let out anger. It is true that if anger explodes uncontrollably it can be counterproductive and we don't get what we need. The world always reflects our actions and if we explode with rage, the world lashes back at us, which causes more distress.

The only real release of anger is to resolve the deeper issues behind it, bring the pain or unhappiness to the surface and use the powerful anger 'energy' to take positive action. We can shout and scream at others but this is futile because it doesn't nurture us. Gone are the days when we had to rage and shout, scream at an empty chair or pummel pillows until we're red in the face. Rage, which is anger that can't be held in any longer, is a child-like reaction to buried anger. One study determined that explosive rage was actually bad for the health because when the participants went into 'a fit of rage' their blood pressure went up and they were more likely to experience heart problems. Lashing out is an inefficient attempt to resolve a problem or make it go away.

Anger is a need that hasn't been met. Therefore we can surmise that the best way of tackling anger is to establish what we need and work from there. I know that when I'm angry and I understand the source of my anger, I can diffuse it by changing something or asking for something. I used to get myself in a tight corner, for example when I did something for someone hoping that they would see me as a 'hero'. And they didn't; they didn't even say thanks! Of course, I'd set myself up to feel bad because I'd assumed they would say thanks and appreciate me.

In this situation I had two choices: one, ask the person if they liked what I did, or two, give myself the praise I was after. Either way, I acknowledged my resentment but I did something about it. I didn't sit on it until it built into a volcano of anger. Many of us who suffer from depression are people-pleasers who want and need recognition but think we never get it. Tackling the themes around anger is probably the one most important issue we can do to help ourselves. There is a specific activity (*Activity 3*) in the following section to help tackle buried anger.

Many of us have anger about our past. We think about it over and over again. But this is only a thought, or a series of thoughts – though very destructive. The memory of the past is what we think happened – but it's gone now and we can release the precious energy it takes to maintain a hold on it. We can't ever resolve our past but with mindful acceptance we can use our anger to clear up issues we have today. If we have current resentments about someone, we can feel the fire of our anger and channel it to find a resolution. For example, if I feel angry with a friend for not returning my calls, instead of falling into the victim role I leave a message on her phone asking her why she hasn't returned my calls. In the past, before I had this insight, I would have seethed about it for days until I finally deduced that it was because I wasn't worth calling back! That's how the anger turned in on me. And then I couldn't speak to her for months. Lost the friend as well! Ouch! So painful. Now I can feel angry but take action without trying to destroy the other person.

We can use acceptance as a way of releasing resentments long before they boil up to become anger. Buddhists say that 'peace is the true path of the warrior' and if we use the sword, we've lost from the start. We don't want to lose sight of our anger but we do want to transform it into a powerful force to help lift us out of depression. Gandhi said 'I have learned through bitter experience the one supreme lesson to conserve my anger and, as heat conserved is transmitted into energy, even so our anger controlled can be transmitted into a power that can move the world.' It is possible to pull our anger out of us like we might raise a pop-up exhibition banner and clip it on the top hook. There it is – powerful anger that we can use to our advantage, standing tall and strong! What would your banner say on it? I would like mine to say 'Here's Alex's strength. It's looking after her. And getting her needs met!' We don't want to remove our anger, we want to make it useful. Sometimes we need anger to deal with angry people. We're not passive, we need to stand up for ourselves. But we don't want it to destroy us. We want it to move mountains.

ACTIVITIES

By completing these three activities and doing them on a regular basis we will begin to clear the backlog of feelings that have built up. Once we start to feel 'lighter' and have fewer burdens there will be two gifts: one is that the depression will lift, and the second is that we will begin to touch the natural state of joy that is waiting for us beneath the buried feelings. An awakening of the heart will begin

Activity 1: Naming feelings

One of the techniques some of us who've suffered from long-term depression have got used to is bundling our feelings up together until they look like a ball of tightly bound rubber bands. It's time to take stock and tease out the rubber bands and identify individual feelings. However, you may find difficulty naming your feelings if you have numbed out over a number of years.

To help you get started, below is a list of feelings with a clear description:

- **Love:** lightness in the body, feeling listened to, a warmth in the heart, feeling valued and understood and safe with another person.
- **Anger:** having a tight jaw, sensing a clenching energy in the chest, pupils dilated, having racing thoughts.
- **Fear:** having a pounding heartbeat, feeling extremely alert, skin going hot or cold and tight rapid breathing.
- **Guilt:** a sense of regret for doing something wrong, being neglectful of another person.
- **Shame:** a feeling of being broken, a burning sensation in the tummy, a sense that the body is shrinking, spiralling down, throat is constricted, speaking is difficult, breathing is difficult, heaviness on the chest. (NB: Guilt is regret about something we have done whereas shame is feeling bad about who we are.)
- **Happiness:** when you feel like smiling, a very light feeling of being in good humour and good spirits.

- **Grief:** a feeling that something has been taken away, yearning for something that has gone, a sense that the crying will never stop, a feeling of disorientation.
- **Abandonment:** a sense of being left out, pushed out, forgotten, minimized, vulnerable and betrayed, feeling like a dot on the horizon, feeling tiny and lost.
- **Hope:** a trust in ourselves and the world that things will work out, energy level rising and life hitting all the positives, breathing easier and lighter.
- **Embarrassed:** feeling exposed, vulnerable, ridiculed, confronted, which makes us feel flushed and hot, feeling red in the face, stomach butterflies and faltering breathing.
- **Humiliation:** a sense of being abused, someone has stolen something from us, our self-respect has deserted us.
- **Betrayed:** feeling deceived, an inward spiralling feeling that depletes us of energy, no trust left in anything or anyone.
- **Inspired:** feeling light and energetic, able to overcome any problem, finding a solution, a sense of wonder, seeing the world in Technicolour.
- **Satisfaction:** a sense of being completely full and restored, being rooted in the body and the body being rooted in the ground, not needing to be elsewhere.
- **Joy:** a sense of feeling like the inside of us matches the outside, inner peace, we have what we need, believing in the abundance of the universe, and that all we need will come to us, energized but calm, warm and light, seeing others in the same way and feeling their light connecting to our light.

Pick out three feelings that dominate you. If you don't think you experience feelings, think about something, like a movie or a song, that caused emotion to stir up in you and use those feelings for this activity. Open your journal and write the answer to these questions about the three feelings:

- Identify feeling in my body:
- Measure depth of feeling on a scale of 1–10
- Reminds me of when . . .
- Open my heart and accept this feeling

Next to each of the three feelings, answer each question. Here's an example:

	Identify feeling in my body	Emphasis scale 1–10	Reminds me of when . . .	How can I open my heart and accept then release this feeling?
Grief	A deep sensation in my chest	8	Feeling lost and abandoned as a child	Imagine it flying out of me
Frustration	A hotness in my head	7	None of my family would talk to me	Thump a pillow and then it will go
Joy	Deep in my stomach – a warm glow	If I focus on it a 6	I had nothing to worry about	I don't want to release it!

Identify your feeling and then score its intensity. Then try to identify what it reminds you of in the past. It's been said that if you experience a feeling for more than 15 minutes then its roots are buried in the past. By discovering, uncovering and accepting this, you will find it easy to move beyond any distress this feeling creates. Repeat this activity once a day in your journal. You will find that, over time, you will come to identify your feelings quickly and easily. By accepting and reuniting with them you are accepting and reuniting with your true self.

Activity 2: Being objective about your feelings

Take a moment to pick out the most painful feeling that comes to mind, one that really sinks you. Now imagine you've picked up that feeling with both hands and placed it on a table. Answer these questions:

- What shape is it?
- How big is it?
- What colour is it?
- Where does it usually live in your body?
- What effect does it have on your body?
- If you hold it in your hand, what does it feel like?

The next questions are the most important. They are about the *resistance* you have about your painful feeling:

- Where does your resistance towards that feeling live in your body?
- What shape is it?
- How big is it?
- What colour is it?
- What effect does it have on your body?
- If you hold it in your hand, what does it feel like?

How does the resistance feel towards your painful feeling? Hate, aggression, rejection? The resistance is causing you the most pain, not the feeling itself. Can you make a decision to welcome the feeling back into your body, no matter how painful it is? Can you accept it without judgement or criticism? It is a part of you and it belongs to you for a reason. For now all you have to do is accept it without resisting it. The feeling will be accepted and this will make you feel better, faster.

Activity 3: A special activity to heal anger

Buried anger is the most likely cause of depression. Many of us don't actually realize or even believe we're angry. Anger can be disguised in many forms but it is usually buried deep in anyone who suffers from depression. Here's a list of symptoms of buried anger:

- Chronic pain in the neck or jaw.
- Sarcasm
- Ironic humour
- Boredom, apathy, disinterest, can't be bothered
- Nightmares

- Smiling when you don't want to
- Controlling your voice
- Grinding your teeth at night
- Becoming irritated at irrelevant things
- Body tics or spasmodic movements that you are unaware of
- Stomach ulcers
- Constant cheerfulness and 'grin and bear it' attitude
- Refusing eye contact
- Clenching a thumb in a fist
- Over politeness
- Not sleeping, or sleeping too much
- Frustration at everything around you
- A feeling that life's not good enough

If you see three or more that apply to you, the chances are that you suffer from buried anger. Buried anger usually covers a loss. Anger and loss go hand in hand. To relieve you of the burden of buried anger it's important to link it to the appropriate loss and the relief will be immediate. Here's the activity to do that:

In your journal write these four headings:

I am angry about	Because	It affects me by	The loss underneath the anger is

An example:

I am angry about	Because	It affects me by	The loss underneath the anger is
The way my friend has treated me over me not taking part in his football weekend.	I have tried to make things right by getting someone to fill in for me; I couldn't go because I knew I would end up abusing myself with alcohol.	Making me feel like I've done something wrong but I haven't – I'm only human and right now I have to put myself first and I can't assume responsibility for sorting out his weekend.	That I'm afraid he won't like and respect me any more; well, let's face it, he hasn't spoken to me for a week!

Once the anger and loss are identified, lots of choices emerge. In this example I can praise myself for doing what felt right for me rather than people-pleasing my friend and ending up feeling resentful. I can stop beating myself up with critical thoughts. I can tell him that I don't like the way he has treated me after I didn't do what he wanted. I can say I didn't want to come because I don't like football.

The journey

Our feeling-recovery journey restores our inner faith that we are OK. The journey is like peeling an onion: there are layers to go through. Some bring tears and some bring a clean skin. This will bring us balance. Anger and grief are the two sources of healing. We discover that we aren't bad people. We are simple human beings who want to make things right and move forward. This feeling work will help us do this. We are gentle with ourselves but we don't make excuses for acting out in harmful ways. We pray for help to stop judging ourselves. We start to forgive ourselves and begin to see light at the end of the tunnel.

Meditation to explore difficult feelings

Settle down in a comfortable chair sitting upright with your feet on the floor. Make sure you are in a room where you can't be disturbed.

> Now bring your attention to your breath . . . . and feel the rise and fall of the abdomen as your breath moves in and out. Sit here for a moment and let your breath be your guide . . . . As you breathe in and out . . . . you may notice your mind is wandering off in thoughts . . . . or that you experience physical sensations in your body . . . . Instead of trying to control these thoughts and sensations . . . . bring your attention into your body and become aware of the physical sensations in your body . . . . These sensations may be very, very subtle . . . . or they may be very strong . . . . It's of no consequence how these physical sensations present

themselves to you . . . . only that you bring your awareness to them and allow your conscious self simply to become attentive to them . . . . Bring your mind now to the sensation that stands out over all the other sensations . . . . Find the place in your body where the strongest sensation manifests itself . . . . Take your awareness from your abdomen into the part of the body where this strong sensation is sitting . . . . The idea is not to change the feeling but to notice it . . . . and become aware of it . . . . If you can isolate the feeling then notice how your breath flows into the sensation and flows out of the sensation . . . . When that sensation has become less significant . . . . move your attention to another sensation you feel in another part of you . . . . As your mind wanders through this meditation become aware of the physical sensations that happen in your body as a result of your thoughts . . . . As each thought takes your attention you may feel a corresponding sensation . . . . simply bring your attention to the sensation and create a space around it allowing it to be . . . . and allowing it to be present in your body in this moment . . . . And as each sensation fades away, bring your attention to other parts of your body that may hold feelings . . . . These feelings are seeking your attention. They want to be accepted so they can be released . . . . Spend a few moments now bringing your attention to all parts of your body where there may be sensations . . . . As you come to the end of this meditation you know you can come back to this place at any time . . . . and become acquainted with the feelings that are waiting for your attention and for your release.

AFFIRMATIONS

I have feelings but I'm not my feelings. Today I can let my feelings come and go. If I feel sad today I will remember that the feeling will pass and I will smile again. I have the power to choose to remember that my feelings are temporary, like passing clouds in the sky and that I can be separate from those clouds and watch them pass.

I am beginning to realize that my feelings are nothing to be afraid of. They can't hurt me or anyone else. I no longer need to deny myself my feelings. I have always judged myself harshly for my feelings but today I will cease. My feelings are unique to me and I will respect them as I learn about them, meet them and then release them.

I respect my feelings today. They make up patterns which, when put together, create a unique me, like a box of puzzle pieces which, when put together, make a beautiful picture. Today I appreciate the beautiful picture made from my feelings and me.

Discovering Your Inner Child

And your new, loving parent

Each of us is composed of two fundamental parts: an inner child and an inner parent. Bringing together these two parts of your soul will help you feel whole again. You may well have some resistance to this idea – in fact it may bring up all kinds of defences – so let me explain a bit further.

Our inner child

Inside of every one of us lives a child. Children are naturally joyful. If you look at the behaviour of children around you they are generally laughing, exploring, running, shouting and screaming with delight. True joy is what children express when they're happy. We did this too when we were young and we still have the potential to feel as joyful as those children, but we may have 'de-pressed' our natural joy and aliveness with layers of unexpressed feelings. They've had nowhere to go except on top of the pile of other emotions and now we're left with an emotional 'compost heap' all steaming and stagnant. However, by reconnecting with our inner child we can work through those layers, throw them off and find our way to the treasure underneath – our natural joy.

The 'child' in us holds all our feelings but if those feelings are painful, we shut down that part of us by 'numbing out' or we use compulsive behaviour as a distraction. It's a natural coping tactic that you can see children using every day. Think of a child who has a hard time at school or at home; can you sense their disengagement? They may be getting themselves into trouble or seem withdrawn or unavailable to play with other kids. They are protecting themselves until they feel safe and can open up and drop their mask. As adults we use this same coping mechanism. When 'stuff' happens we shut down or distract ourselves from the feelings which are too painful to work through. But when we feel safer those feeling begin to emerge. They didn't go anywhere but were waiting to be let out.

We can come out from our hiding place and become willing and ready to let go of our negative feelings. All we need is to be heard and have our feelings understood. It's been said that when families go into therapy, it's the children who 'get it' first; 'it' being understanding that other people's problems are not their problems and that they themselves are OK. The adults have years of conditioning to get through but the children are closer to their real selves. This helps to explain why we can beat depression faster by reconnecting with the inner child.

The mere mention of the term 'inner child' may make you cringe and run for cover. I know this was the case for me. I was scared of uncovering this part of me. I felt ashamed because it was where I stored my secrets, the things I would never tell anyone else and the shameful habits which I couldn't bear anyone else to see.

Connecting with your inner child might leave you feeling vulnerable and having to acknowledge how defenceless and helpless you feel. This could feel risky and dangerous. However, it is possible to work through these feelings to uncover a healthier relationship with the inner child.

This inner child *is real*. Not literally. Nor physically. But psychologically real. And powerful. Most psychologists agree that many mental disorders and destructive behaviour patterns are related in some degree to this unconscious part of us. We were all once children, and still have that child living within us, though most people are quite unaware of this. And this lack of conscious relatedness to our own inner child is precisely where so many behavioural, emotional and relationship difficulties stem from.

The fact is that the majority of so-called grown-ups are not truly grown up at all. We all get older but, psychologically speaking, this is not adulthood. True adulthood hinges on acknowledging, accepting, and taking responsibility for loving and parenting our own inner child. For many grown-ups, this never happens. Instead, their inner child has been denied, neglected, bullied, abandoned or rejected. We are told by society to grow up and put childish ways aside. To become adults, we've been taught that our inner child, representing our child-like capacity for innocence, wonder, awe and joy, must be stifled, isolated and repressed. However, the inner child comprises and harnesses these positive qualities.

The inner child also holds our accumulated childhood pain, traumas, fears and anger. Adults are convinced they have successfully outgrown this child and their emotional baggage long ago. But this is far from the truth. If we are depressed then often inside us is a wounded and angry child running around in an adult body, like a hurting six-year-old in a grown-up suit, making decisions and trying to get by in the world. How can we have a grown-up relationship with anyone or a golden career or raise our own children into happy healthy adults when we're carrying around a hurt and frightened child?

If you think about it, wouldn't any child having to fend for themselves feel the same way without proper support? It's a confusing state of affairs and why so many of us look for help. What we need help with is to bring together and identify the unconscious part of us that is our inner child so that we can attend to the unmet needs of that child. Once our inner child is heard, loved, accepted, nurtured and protected we liberate it and this is where true freedom lies. So how do we do this?

Our new, loving parent

The gateway to healing the inner child is to discover our new parent. Our biological parents were the ones responsible for making us and raising us but now we need to release our biological parents and find a new parent inside us – the one who is connected to our higher power. Easily said, but how is this done? Well, this isn't as weird as it sounds because we already parent ourselves, but perhaps not in a way that helps us feel happy. If we are depressed then we are obeying a harsh inner voice that we've developed over time; it is hounding us and pushing us into depression. To beat depression fast we can turn that voice around to become the loving parent we've always yearned for.

Reliving forgotten memories

Ground-breaking research from the 1950s demonstrated that by touching a part of the brain (the temporal cortex) with a weak electrical probe, the brain could be caused to 'play back' certain past experiences, and the feelings associated with them. When certain events were 'replayed' the research volunteers had associated feelings to do with these events despite *not being able to remember them*. The widely accepted conclusion to these studies was that our brains act as recording machines. The brain has recorded an experience even though we may have *no memory of it*. However, we vividly connect to the associated feelings that we had at the time of the experience, in spite of not remembering it.

To beat depression fast we need to learn how to stop responding to old experiences. New rules and beliefs need to be put in place. A new response to our childhood needs to be developed and new anchors need to be fixed. This is done through guided mediation and the activities that follow later in this chapter. This gets to the core of our internal beliefs and challenges them faster than any other therapeutic technique possible. It gets into the engine, cleans it and adjusts the cogs so it can work to its full potential.

Our inner child has most likely developed ways to protect itself and this may have led us to sabotaging relationships with other people because we were so deeply ashamed about who we were. I know I developed a feeling of deep isolation, firmly believing that no one could help me get better. By developing our own loving parent we can begin the healing and put the shattered pieces back together.

A *loving* parent

All of us have a loving voice inside. Even in the worst periods of depression we can always awaken that tiny voice. This is the voice of our loving parent. Our new parent can help us challenge the old, critical voice to care for our inner child better. We can learn to re-parent ourselves and lose interest in compulsive behaviour that only harms us. We can learn to give ourselves a sense of worth, something that may be lacking when we're in the depths of depression.

When our loving parent starts to care for our inner child we begin to understand the motivation for some of our behaviour. Our parent can help to change our responses for our own good. We start to employ the loving parent by listening to how we speak to ourselves. Once we begin doing this we will start to hear the judgements. Some of us may not hear them clearly to begin with because they work like the hum of a refrigerator in the background. We're so used to them we only recognize them when they've been turned off. However, once we can hear the critic, it's like finding the end in a ball of tangled wool and we can follow the rest of the thread until we untangle the whole ball.

I know you are reading this book because you want to beat depression – fast – but some aspects of recovery take time. You didn't get depressed in a day and you won't recover in a day. The process is simple – a series of steps – but it is important to give yourself time to take small steps in the journey to healing the inner child.

It is important to be loving and gentle and to put some support in place. You might consider joining a self-help group, a visit to the doctor, or counselling. This is the time to ask for help from your higher power, your loving parent, and other supportive people. I know that picking up the phone or reaching out to others isn't easy. It takes courage to take that first step. But you will certainly reap the rewards.

Becoming the new parent to our inner child means replacing our biological parents with our own set of life rules that nurture the inner child. Our new parent with a loving voice will create a safe place for our inner child to come alive. We can ask our higher power to help us reconnect with that loving voice.

Becoming our inner child's number one fan

Imagining walking through a park and finding a child sitting by a tree with her head down and looking despondent and abandoned. How would you react? If she seemed depressed, confused and anxious or upset, as adults, wouldn't we want to help her and find the compassion to sit down next to her and talk to her, listen to her, hold her in our arms and soothe her until she felt better. Try to see your inner child as a real child standing a few feet away from you. It's so much easier to see how to help him or her.

Like any child who is distressed, our inner child *has to learn to trust* the loving parent. If we are depressed then it's likely that this inner child *doesn't trust us.* And why should they? Perhaps we've been unable to recognize that we have a wounded inner child but now we know that we can begin to be more trustworthy. We have to build trust that we will be there for the child whatever happens. This is the next step to securing a bond between our inner child and our loving parent. The following exercise is designed to help you do that. For ease of writing, I have used the pronoun 'him' but of course I mean him or her.

Say hello

Begin by writing a letter to your inner child. In your journal write the letter with your dominant hand. Introduce yourself and explain all about your life now and your pleasure at having your inner child in your life. Tell him how much you want to have him with you always and how you want to help him feel better, grow stronger and become happy. You can tell him you've been waiting for him and that you're glad you can see each other.

Then allow the child to respond to the adult's letter in your non-dominant hand and see what emerges.

Tell him how strong you are

If a child knows your adult strengths they will feel more secure. This is an opportunity to tell your inner child what your strengths are. Write a list of all the things you can do as an adult that you couldn't do when you were a child. Write it so a child would understand it. These could be things like: I have a job which pays the bills, I own a car and I can drive it. I have money in the bank. I can come home at whatever time I like. I can eat what I want, and so on.

Allow the child to ask you questions in your non-dominant hand and see what emerges.

Tell your child about your higher power

Make it fun. Children love fun – and magic. Explain the enormous supremacy of your higher power. Tell your child how this power is always, always, there for both of you. Show him how you ask your higher power for things you want. Tell your child how your higher power has given you things you have asked for. Make your child aware that this loving power is there to help both of you come together and make it possible for you (the adult) always to be there for the child.

Let the child express his awe at such an amazing thing.

Ask your inner child for forgiveness

You want to make sure the child knows you are aware that he's been neglected over the years. Ask him for his forgiveness. Writing a letter in your dominant hand is the best way to do this. Explain to your child how you know you've neglected him and haven't always been there for him. Or that your attention has often been elsewhere but that's changed and you would like the child's forgiveness now.

Allow the child to respond using the non-dominant hand and you may be deeply moved by the response you receive.

Learn to play again

Children ask for very little. They want to be unconditionally loved and, once they have that sorted, they want to play. Our inner child is a fountain of fun. You can give him permission to start playing again. You can find out what fun means for your inner child either by asking him directly or by writing to him. Sometimes you have to set some boundaries –'No, chasing cars is not going to happen, let's chase a kite instead.' But that's about all you have to do. Little by little you can begin to enjoy being with your inner child and your inner child will grow in confidence and trust that you will always be there. Make a list of all the things you loved to do as a child and plan how to do them now. It might be playing on swings, making a sandcastle on the beach, or baking cakes. Children love simple things.

Healing the inner child with new rules

We can heal our inner child by putting some new rules in place. There are two things you can give a child which will last a lifetime: roots and wings. The roots are rules and the wings help them soar. Children need rules to feel safe. Once they feel safe they can break the rules. Once they've broken the rules they've grown their own wings and can fly. Our inner child can't be free until he has safe and respectful rules in place. Rules help us flourish. Imagine a world without them: there would be total chaos. It can be a lot of fun putting in place some new rules for your inner child.

When I first tried this exercise my rules for my inner child looked like this:

1. It's OK to feel how you feel – angry, sad, depressed or happy. All of them are 100% acceptable. You don't need to have any guilt about feelings.
2. It's OK to want things. You may not get everything you want but that doesn't mean you can't ask for it.
3. It's OK to say 'no' to stuff you don't want to do. Sometimes you have to do things you don't want to do, like tidying your room, but that's different. This rule says that if you don't want to help someone or do something that they tell you to do, you don't have to say 'yes' automatically. You can think about it before you decide.

79

4. At the same time you can be respectful of other people's feelings. You can listen and respond without being abusive. You want others to be respectful to you too.

5. It's OK to express your feelings and you can learn to express them in a grown-up way. For example, if you feel angry, you can say 'I feel angry' without acting out the anger.

6. It's OK not to be perfect. No one is perfect and we all have imperfections. I will love you just as much with your imperfections.

7. You will always try be honest But you will be careful what you say to certain people, however. Telling someone you're depressed may not work until you feel safe that whatever they say back won't affect you. This is what you will work towards until you feel so bouncy that you're not afraid to tell the truth.

8. It's OK to make mistakes. Everyone makes mistakes and it's a way of helping us to stay on our true path. You will not be judged for making mistakes.

Write a set of rules for your inner child using the voice of your loving parent.

Connecting our inner child and our loving parent
1: Meeting our inner child visualization

Here is a beautiful visualization to bring together your inner child and your loving parent. You can read through the text and remember the words or you can record the words and take yourself through the visualization, remembering to leave long pauses at each series of dots.

You can do this visualization either sitting or lying down. Begin by finding a comfortable position.

Now close your eyes and become aware of what's going on inside you and your body . . . . Become aware of your breath as it moves into the body . . . . and out of the body . . . . in through the nose . . . . and out through the mouth.... Become aware of the different temperatures of the breath going in.... and the breath going out. And as you notice thoughts simply let them go.... like small white fluffy clouds in a blue sky.... You don't need to respond to any thoughts or sensations.... but simply become aware of them.... and allow space for them.... If you find your attention wanders away with a thought.... simply escort your attention back to your body.... back to your breath.... Bring your awareness back to your breath.... moving in and out of your body.... Notice how your abdomen rises with each breath in.... and returns with each breath out.... Notice how your breath moves in and out effortlessly.... and your abdomen rises up and down effortlessly.... It's with this effortlessness that you allow your thoughts to be released.... like puffy white clouds in a blue sky.... Bring your attention to any tension or stress that is in your body right now.... As you move to a different part of your body simply bring your focus to the tension.... and let it be as it is.... Imagine it dissolving into millions of small beads of light and spiralling into the universe.... Continue with an easy open awareness.... not resisting anything.... and allowing yourself to be in this space.... And now invite your inner child to come to you.... How do you sense this child?.... How old is this child?.... What emotions are you sensing are coming from this child?.... You may remember yourself as a child or you may have a memory of yourself or from a photograph.... Allow that memory to come forwards.... You may see your child.... or you may simply feel the presence of the child.... The child may come to you as a light or a feeling.... or simply an awareness.... You may feel the child in a part of your body.... Become aware of the part of you that senses the presence of this child.... Now you can allow yourself to connect with your inner child . . . . in whatever way feels the right way for you . . . . There is no right or wrong . . . . it is a spontaneous connection and unique to you . . . . You may feel the child as a separate part of you . . . . You may feel you are the child . . . . Your inner child will guide you towards what needs to be held or what needs to be embraced . . . . Simply be with that child . . . . Simply be aware of the essence of the child . . . . Simply notice your responses to the child . . . . Take some time now to ask the inner child some questions . . . . Ask your inner child what they would like from you at this moment. Create a space for the response of the child . . . . Let the child's response be completely spontaneous . . . . Ask the child what would make them feel safe and happy . . . . Take some time to explore the feelings and needs of that child . . . . Be totally present to whatever the child needs at this moment . . . . Ask the child what they want to say to you . . . . Let the flow of the questions happen spontaneously . . . . Ask the child what they need to feel nourished . . . . and how you can help to create a safe place for the child . . . . Allow your loving parent to respond to your inner child in the way that feels perfect to you . . . . Allow your responses to the child to come from a loving place or a higher power within you . . . . You can give that child exactly what they need . . . . Praise the child completely . . . . Tell the child how you love that child beyond words . . . . Feel the space between you and the child as you share your love with them . . . . Bring your attention to the space that is beyond the child and beyond the adult and is connected to something greater which surrounds you . . . . This space around you which holds the child and the parent is filled with light and love and compassion . . . . If your mind begins to judge this moment simply let the judgements float away like white clouds against a blue sky . . . . Simply come back to the presence that holds this inner child and his parent in this moment.... Hold both your inner child and your parent in this light that surround you.... Allow this moment to be the moment for your inner child to tell you what he or she needs at this moment.... And use this time to allow your parent to respond to that child with love and compassion and gentleness and understanding.... And when you want to you can hold your child and can tell the child that you are always there for them.... that you will come back to this place and talk to them whenever the child needs you to.

Reconnecting with the inner child helps us to uncover and understand what we need if we are to feel good and happy. It changes our feelings of isolation to feelings of worth. By regularly doing this visualization it can help replace the feeling of being disconnected with one of feeling whole again.

2: Talking directly to our inner child

This exercise is to help you connect with your inner child through the non-dominant hand writing activity. It's a perfect way for you to check in with your inner child on a daily basis. It helps you to reconnect continually with the child until it becomes an automatic sequence. It will help you to identify how you can take better care of yourself and your inner world.

When you do this you may feel connected to the child in a naïve and compassionate way because of the childish writing he produces. The non-dominant hand writes like a child and seeing the words on the page can help us to soften and care for the child. It can be a humbling and exciting moment the first time you do this. There on the page is a child who was lost and who now is found.

Open your journal so you have two clean pages in front of you and hold a pen in your non-dominant hand. Now let your inner child write something on one page. Interestingly, he will probably have lots to say! Then take the pen in your other hand and write down the response from your adult perspective on the opposite page. Then swap the pen to the non-dominant hand again and follow the conversation through. The writing is another way of 'talking' and caring for the inner child. It's a two-way conversation understood by both parties. Here are some examples of how this activity might develop:

- In the morning you may talk to the child as you would talk to a child before they go to school and discuss things like a certain dream that happened the night before or something particular he wants to pay attention to that day; the parent can respond with reassurance and unconditional love.
- Last thing at night, when the child may need to discuss the day and how he did, the parent can soothe and restore confidence in the child that he is loved and that he did a great job that day.
- To look at how the parent is doing as a loving parent and what different things the child needs from the parent to feel happy.
- Any time there is something that upsets the child like a shock, a family drama or conflict with another person; the parent can assure the child that they are safe and everything will work out.
- If the child is happy he may want to share it with the parent in the same way a child wants to show their parents how high they can climb or fast they can run!

As the loving parent it may be tricky to know what advice and nurturing to give the inner child but that will come with time and is unique to each one of us. If we are guided by our compassionate self then we will find the loving action. It's important this journal is kept safe and that no one will ever read it. This will help your inner child to feel as secure as possible. Privacy when writing is essential too. The inner child may want to cry or get angry. Make sure you have tissues and a cushion to squeeze.

Teddy talk!

Another way to talk to your inner child is to use a teddy. Get an old teddy or something else for your inner child to help you feel his presence. A photograph of yourself as a child may help you to get started if you're really struggling to grasp the idea. Study the photograph and become aware of the responses in your body. This is an indication that the child is there but not willing to come out yet. Give him time and he will emerge.

By using the teddy you brought along for your child, you can open a dialogue with your inner child. If you hold it in front of you, hold it in the non-dominant hand to talk as your child and hold it in the dominant hand to talk as your adult.

Ask your child any question you like while holding the teddy in the dominant hand and while you look at the teddy. Remember this parent is the one who really understands the child's anguish and is there as a compassionate, loving adult who knows there's a good reason for the child's anguish. A simple question might be: how do you feel right now? Then hold the teddy close to your body, particularly your stomach because this is usually where the child lives, and sense any feelings in this area.

Then put the teddy in your non-dominant hand and allow the feelings from the child to come out and let him share how he is feeling with you. Then take the teddy back into the dominant hand and respond to the child as a loving parent. Then move the teddy back to the non-dominant hand again to allow the child to speak again.

Questions the loving parent can ask the inner child:

- Would you like to tell me how you're feeling right now?
- Would you like me to help you understand why you're feeling like that?
- What would you like me to do to help you feel better?
- What is it you fear so that I might be able to help you?
- What would you like to know that will help you feel safer?

You can use this activity to explore the beliefs behind the feelings. As we know, children often feel that things are their fault and this is the perfect time to explain to the child that that's not the case. If the child is angry this is the opportunity for him to express the anger to you. All a child wants is to be heard and have their feelings accepted and that's all you have to do. You can explain to the child that his beliefs are based on something that happened long ago and is not relevant today.

> When I did the dominant and non-dominant hand writing activity a strange revelation came about. I realized that I had always thought my dad left home when I was 11 because of me. On my birthday I received a skateboard but what I wanted was a bike and I made a real fuss about not getting what I wanted. The next day my dad left home and I always thought it was because I made a fuss about not getting a bike. When I did this activity this memory came up and I was really shocked. Because how could a kid be responsible for the break-up of his parents' marriage? I had to do this activity over and over until I really believed it wasn't my fault. And I was so angry about it I couldn't stop thinking that as a kid no one put me right. Even though I spoke to my mum about it she never told me that that wasn't the reason he left home. Now I'm older I can look back and see that she was very depressed and didn't have any time for me. And probably it didn't even occur to her that I took that break-up on my shoulders. But it affected everything I did because I thought that making a fuss about something was a really, really bad thing to do. If I hadn't had done that activity I would never have known that and it's turned my life around. *Sam*

A word about dealing with our parents if we are finding them difficult

Some of you may have had a difficult time with your parents and need some guidance on how to manage this relationship whilst you navigate the choppy waters of depression. Others, however, have no issues with their parents and if that's the case then this section is not relevant to you.

Before we start, it's important to be clear on the effect our biological parents may have had on our well-being today. This is especially true if we believe our parents are to blame for our depression. Many of us have been depressed from childhood and, as a result, find ourselves in a dead-end. We want to blame our parents for what they did to us. We also want them to help us but that's like going back into the lion's den and is not a good place to go for healing. This section is for those of you who know the roots of your depression lie in your childhood.

It's true that our parents' parenting styles may have taught us to feel like victims and *not* how to become assertive and confident. They may simply have been undermining us or they may have been out and out abusive. It's also true that the way they treated us may have left scars in our souls. But from where we stand, here and now, as adults, they cannot help us recover from depression and we can't look to them to help us recover. If we do we go right back, psychologically, to become embroiled in the very parenting that got us here in the first place. When we're depressed we can't help but go back into the role of a child because our defences have left us. Being with our parents *at this point* can set us backwards.

In order to recover faster, you may find it helpful to separate yourself physically and emotionally from your biological parents for a period so you can start your recovery with a clean slate without having to worry about their needs or influence on your well-being. Although studies show that parents and other family members can be very supportive in the recovery from addiction, when it comes to long-term depression, it is different. By returning to our parents, who may have taught us how to suppress our needs and feelings, we continue the pattern of behaviour that set us on the path towards depression.

Here are some ideas that may help you to get some distance:

- Spend less time with your parents.
- Remind yourself that your parents were responsible for how you were brought up but *you are responsible for your life from today onwards.*
- Learn to say no to your parents when they want something from you that would cost you dearly; for example if they want your time to help them with their lives but it costs you in buried resentment then you have to learn to say no.
- Turn inappropriate guilt into self-reassurance; if parents cry 'but we never see you', turn the automatic guilt into a new thought or say *that's because I need to build my own life and recover from this depression.*
- Spend time with your parents on your terms, not theirs
- Learn to challenge their old ways if appropriate; for example if a mother turns the subject around to her in every conversation then say 'if I can get back to what I was saying Mum'.
- Get your needs met elsewhere and don't just crawl back to them when you feel depressed – oh, so easy to do on a bad day!

You don't need to cut out your parents completely from your life. What is helpful is to be aware of how needy you may be for your parents' approval. Journal writing and discussions with others will help you to identify how you may still be looking for the parental green light. The ten steps described in this book will help you to find how you've adapted old family rules for yourself and how you can put in place new rules to help you to feel better and recover from depression.

All of this can be done without the input of parents. This may seem like an extreme approach but consider this: if we went to our parents and told them how depressed we were and how we think that they did certain things that may have contributed to our depression today, what response would we get? If we have parents who can't take responsibility for their actions we might get one of the following:

- I don't remember what you're talking about.
- I did it for your own good.
- Please don't be angry with me.
- You have no idea what I was going through at the time.
- How dare you be ungrateful.
- Pull your socks up and stop feeling sorry for yourself.

If we are fortunate enough to have parents who take full responsibility for their actions, we may get the following response:

- We were not good parents when we were younger.
- I know exactly what you're talking about and I beg your forgiveness.
- I recognize I did my best but it wasn't good enough for you.

Either way, not one of these responses is going to take away your depression today. Even if your parents were fully qualified, top of their game therapists who help others recover from deep emotional traumas every day of their working lives, they cannot help you recover from depression. Our recovery needs to be conducted away from the environment we were raised in if we want to recover from depression *faster*. We simply have to stop *looking to them to fix us.* That is an emotional separateness which is necessary to become autonomous.

It's not easy for us to step away from our parents even if it's temporary. If we're chronically depressed the chances are that we haven't fully separated from them in a way that we don't even understand. For instance, if we're still seeking their approval or if we fear their reproach then we're still attached to them. Our depression may simply be as a result of not feeling completely adult yet, somehow still stuck to the old family rules.

There is hope, however, by following the steps given here. These steps teach us how to find our true adult selves and once we begin to feel the amazing power of self-reliance and real autonomy, we find it easier to go back to our parents and see them for who they really are: the people who gave birth to us, to whom we owe nothing but whom we can love with an open heart. It can feel painful to step away from the parental umbrella, it may seem like the road less travelled, but this road is the one that will take us to new beginnings and help us to heal the depression fast – and for good.

AFFIRMATIONS FOR THE INNER CHILD

I've never met another child like you; you are perfect just the way you are and I will love you for ever.

I've prepared a special place for you to live with me and all your needs will be met.

I want to look after you for ever and I'm prepared to do whatever it takes to make sure you are happy.

Whatever you're feeling, I accept it. Whatever you need, I accept it. Whatever you do, I accept it.

Healing Toxic Shame

And discovering real freedom

Toxic shame comes as part of the package of depression. Some experts would suggest that shame is at the root of all depression. Essentially shame is when we feel brutally bad about the person we are. It's when we feel the agony of acute self-consciousness. We feel so awful we have to disown the part of ourselves that holds the shame. We may feel so ashamed about ourselves that we have to hide it from everyone, which makes us ashamed about our shame. We have to keep it a secret and because our shame is so toxic, we spend the whole time running away from it.

Let's start by differentiating between shame and guilt: guilt is a feeling we get when we think that we *did* something bad. Shame is a feeling we get that we *are* simply just a bad person, regardless of anything we did, and nothing can be done about it.

The good news is that shame is a learned habit and can be un-learned. Recovering our sense of self by diminishing and healing the part of us that feels the toxic shame will help us to become whole again. By accepting and reuniting with this hidden self we touch the core of the depression and learn how to overcome this toxic shame habit. This helps us beat depression faster by cutting through the layers to the roots of the problem.

Healthy shame

It's difficult to define shame because originally it was a healthy emotion. People who do not suffer from depression allow shame to work in their lives. Shame in its pure sense is a stabilizer and helps us to recognize when we've made a mistake. It's also a catalyst for us to take responsibility and put the mistake right. Shame is particularly helpful for children. It helps a child to understand the difference between right and wrong.

Healthy shame works like a set of traffic lights: the bigger the mistake the more vibrant the red light. Healthy children come to rely on shame to tell them how far to go. Shame tells us when we've gone far enough and when it's time to make tracks back again. It allows us to make amends for our mistakes, say sorry and never feel bad about doing that. For adults shame is a moral compass showing us what's appropriate and what is discouraged. Our shame tells us that it's not good to steal something from the office or cheat in an exam. It helps us stay on the straight and narrow, own up and be honest.

Toxic shame

Toxic shame, however, is a very different matter. This type of shame is at the heart of depression. It's a feeling of not being good enough, feeling unacceptable and feeling that the very centre of us is *rotten to the core*. Toxic shame is a life-destroying poison that eats away at our soul, telling us that everything we do is a mistake, everything we say is a mistake and in fact we are a mistake. It's very secretive and prefers its host to keep it hidden away from anyone else. If we make a small mistake, shame will tell us that we are useless, flawed and a failure. It tells us we have no rights, no value and are completely unlovable.

What does shame feel like?

To be absolutely clear, shame is a belief, not a feeling. It permeates feelings and thoughts – not just some of them but *all* of them. This is why the term 'shame-based' is used to describe the thoughts and feelings of someone in this state The shame-based person doesn't question the shame because shame makes them not value themselves enough to accept any alternatives. It's only when we get some help or become aware that there is such a thing that we can become aware of our shame. Until then we may only recognize that we're depressed and not know exactly why. Because exposure of the shame is too much to bear, we hide it. But then something happens to trigger the shame and it can cause immense suffering, like a raw open wound that anyone can rub salt in. We feel totally at the mercy of other people. What might be an off-the-cuff comment from someone can make us feel so ashamed that we want to run away and go into hiding permanently.

Where does it come from?

Essentially toxic shame is handed down from one generation to the next. Critical messages that are shelled out to the children in the family are always bound up in a blanket of shame.

- You can't do anything right.
- Who do you think you are, talking to me like that?
- I would never say anything like that to my mother when I was your age.
- What's wrong with you, why can't you do anything I ask?

It's not so much *what* is said to a child, it's the implicated shame that's the issue. If our parents are saturated with toxic shame (and have not done their own recovery work) they will pass on that shame to the child. No matter how the parent tries *not to pass on* the shame, *it's impossible* to stop it going from one generation to the next.

How does shame manifest in us?

It's vital to challenge toxic shame. I know, because I have been down this path. My toxic shame caused me to hold a powerful belief that I was truly and honestly a bad person. I was terrified of exposure, even if it looked like another person might understand my feelings. Instead I isolated myself. It's completely illogical because somehow I thought that other people had a right to feel

OK about themselves but for some reason I didn't! I suffered burning, excruciating humiliation just for being the person I was. Toxic shame made me feel like I was dirty, and not just in things related to sex, but in everything about me. Because of this belief everything about me had to be kept a secret. The main secret I kept from others was that I was unlovable. Toxic shame made me needy and clingy because I was so desperately trying to feel lovable. As a result I struggled in intimate relationships.

Here are some other indicators of toxic shame:

- Swinging from feeling helpless and hopeless to feeling uncontrollable rage
- Strong need to control – controlling urges are a compensation for feeling a lack of self-worth
- Keeping the lack of self-worth a secret – shame hates being exposed
- Not being in touch with needy feelings – too shameful
- Secretly criticizing others – projecting self-shame onto other people, which brings temporary relief
- Being dependent on behaviours that bring temporary relief like compulsive need for sex, excessive drinking and working, shopping, porn addiction, etc.
- Self-harming as a way of acting out self-hating
- Not sharing inner turmoil with anyone
- Unable to maintain eye contact
- Apologizing a lot
- Rescuing others as a way of trying to feel more in control
- Being high achievers as a way of trying to 'prove' self-worth
- Procrastinating because of not feeling worth it
- Arguing a lot – a way of justifying the shame
- Inflexibility – the shame won't allow doubt
- Swinging from 'everyone loves me' to 'everybody hates me'
- Hopelessness because the shame is so embedded it almost feels impossible to escape it

- Extreme arrogance as a way of trying to stay one step ahead of the shame

If you identify with three of these indicators then you probably suffer from toxic shame. The biggest stumbling block preventing the healing of toxic shame is failing to acknowledge it. It's so shaming to accept we have this demon inside us, but when we do we can breathe easy because now we have something we can work with to beat the depression faster.

Defences against shame

If we suffer from rampant toxic shame we have to find ways to defend ourselves against it.

One of my defences against shame was to think I was 'special and different' to everyone else, that my problems were like no one else's problems and that no one else could understand what I was going through. Unfortunately this had the effect of keeping me isolated and lonely. Of course I'm human and have ups and downs like everyone else. I'm really no different or more special than the rest of the human race. But when I'm hiding from toxic shame, I go into this magical world which makes me feel cut off from others. It's an egotistical way of seeing myself but it was developed at a young age. I now know when I'm running from toxic shame and I can talk about it rather than isolate myself from others. This has helped me beat depression faster. I can't afford to ignore shame so I make sure I open up whenever it hits me. I now laugh at it, and myself, whenever I go into a shame cycle.

How to heal toxic shame – fast

Rest assured you don't have to revisit your earliest childhood memories exhaustively to start healing toxic shame. However, some work on examining how you were brought up will be helpful. People who carry toxic shame are often saddled with the 'don't talk, don't trust, don't feel' rule, likely learned in childhood and taught to the child to keep the family shame a secret. This secrecy is the insidious enemy to healing shame. Trying to overcome this secrecy can feel deeply and profoundly wrong because we learnt it at such an early age. But the irony is that the very thing that toxic shame hides from – exposure – is the only way to heal it.

When I suffered from shame, I spent a lot of time trying not to feel how I felt, trying to climb out of my skin, run from my issues and distract myself from my inner pain, yet I felt powerless because none of these approaches worked. I didn't believe I deserved a place in this world. Until I stopped to address the root cause of my pain – the shame itself – I kept running.

In this section we use acceptance and mindfulness to heal the toxic shame. And expose it.

Expose it? You're kidding me!?

That's right. Exposing the shame *is* the fastest way to beat it.

Much work has been done in the world of Positive Psychology to show us how identifying the shaming voice and its destructiveness can neutralize its negative influence *fast*. Bringing it to the surface gives us back our power. This lessens its effects and changes it into a more positive and non-critical voice. As the self-harm lessens, the healing begins.

But it's important to take baby steps as you begin this process. For now, you probably only want to disclose toxic shame to yourself. You may decide that once you've mastered little areas of shame you may want to find others to share bigger chunks of shame with. When you are ready, seeking some extra help through a counsellor or group would be extremely valuable to tackle all of the core toxic shame.

In this next activity we look at our shame, how it's kept us in the dark and how we can change our self-image. By throwing light on the shame it will automatically dissolve.

The shame loop

At the moment what probably happens if you're very depressed is that you get caught in a shame loop:

Shame about
who we are

Hiding it
through
defensive
behaviour

Feelings of
shame deepen

The shame loop is something we have got tangled in. It's like being in a trance where the exit door is simply a misty mirage in the haze. Or like being stuck in a swamp where no matter how hard we try to get out, the mud sucks us back in. The 'negative' feelings not only make us feel depressed but they feed the shame which tells us how bad we are.

Often we act out in ways that create toxic shame when what we actually want is to be close to others. We all have a yearning to connect and belong. When we ignore these needs, our inner child will act out in ways that don't work. Then shame becomes even more toxic. It's like we're saying to ourselves: 'You don't deserve closeness with others,' and this makes us feel desperately lonely. Once the pain of loneliness increases we have to isolate and protect ourselves. But, after time, what once worked no longer serves us and we simply increase our sense of deficiency until we feel – well, empty.

Loneliness combined with the fear of being close is where the two extremes of shame come together. We yearn for the intimacy of a relationship but we're too ashamed to be vulnerable. Intimacy requires us to risk opening up and talking about who we are, what we feel and think at a deep level. To be intimate is to accept ourselves and others without criticism. However, when we are riddled with shame, this is impossible because we're hiding from ourselves as well as others. When we're ashamed we reject ourselves with contempt and disgust. How could we expect a healthy, intimate relationship with anyone when we cannot love and accept ourselves? Now is the time to challenge these old ways and beat a new path to happiness.

Getting a new perspective on our toxic shame

In this activity you will have a grid with four columns. Draw a table with these headings in your journal:

What happened	How it made me feel ashamed	What I would say to a child	The adult perspective

In the first column you identify something that *happened* that left you feeling ashamed. In the second column you write *how* it made you feel ashamed. In the third column you take a step back and imagine the same thing happening to a small child and *what you would say* to that child. And in the fourth column you neutralize the shame by writing a more *adult perspective* on the incident.

Here are some simple examples:

What happened	How it made me feel ashamed	What I would say to a child	The adult perspective
I went to a party in the wrong clothes.	I felt like I stuck out.	It doesn't matter what clothes you wore you look gorgeous in whatever you wear.	Other adults don't take much notice what other people wear.
I shouted at someone in the street.	I felt like a shit afterwards even though I was angry.	OK, you were angry but it's OK to be angry with someone. We're all angry sometimes, it doesn't make you bad.	It was an exchange – no one was hurt and it could be the rage of the inner child spilling out. Time to delve in and discover how to express anger so you don't feel ashamed.

| I spent too much money and I can't pay my bills. | I feel hopeless and helpless. Useless and pathetic. | You're not a useless person; you may be spending to try and cover your pain which is a normal human thing to do. | When I spend money I don't have it's because I'm trying to numb out. I'll take myself off to have some free fun instead. I'll go to the park whenever I feel the urge to spend. |
| I've had sex with someone when I didn't want to. | I feel dirty, filthy and ugly. | Having sex with that person does not make you bad. Maybe you wanted to be touched but not to have sex and you couldn't ask. | I need some emotional intimacy, not sex. Time to find someone to share with and ask for a hug. |

To heal our toxic shame the only way out is to go through it! We have to come out of hiding and embrace it. Shame lives in a dark place but by shining a light on it, we expose it. This may feel painful – and this is what we try to avoid – pain! But how long have we been trying to avoid this pain? *For ever!* And what's the result? *Depression!* It's been said that all emotional illness is caused by avoiding this pain and the more we avoid it, the worse it gets.

> I found taking the first step the hardest. I'd told a woman in a group I went to that I was scared of the other women. At the time that was about the most excruciating thing I'd ever said to someone else (looking back I can't quite believe it). She said 'they are all pussycats underneath!' and thought no more of it. I thought she was going to tell me how pathetic I was but she didn't. My confidence went up a little. So I started sharing other anecdotes about what I thought and each time I felt a little easier. After that I was on a roll. I now find it very easy to admit when I feel shameful about something. In the last seven days I've owned up to feeling fat and ugly when I was shown a picture of Sharon Stone (same age as me), when I stole a chocolate

bar from the shop, feeling like a fraud when I cancelled dinner for friends because I couldn't be bothered and how shitty I felt when I sold a car with dodgy brakes. All these things I shared with a good friend. There was a time when I would have died (literally) rather than share what seemed like awful secrets. Nowadays I roll with the punches and they just don't bother me any more. I know when I've done wrong but I don't beat myself up. I've accepted the guilt and decided not to do it again – if that makes sense? *Deborah*

Some Guidance

1. Understand that shame tactics are learned – not who YOU are.
2. Learn to love the small part of you who's been in hiding for so long.
3. Share, honestly, with others you feel safe with.
4. Identify how you avoid others because of your shame.
5. Build self-esteem.
6. Be vigilant about which situations trigger toxic shame.
7. Be 100% honest with yourself about parts of you that make you feel ashamed.
8. Learn how to assert yourself with people who make you feel ashamed.
9. Stop using criticizing language to yourself.
10. Ask for help from your higher power to guide you.

ACTIVITIES

Dissolving shame with mindfulness and acceptance: The hand on the heart activity

To disentangle ourselves from this shame loop, here is an activity drawn from mindfulness-based cognitive therapy and the idea of 'radical acceptance'. These two approaches to dissolve shame can be practised every day or at least whenever we feel the shame. It has been shown that shame can be experienced simply as an embedded memory stimulus which can be challenged so that it no longer takes over our whole being. We will then begin to see the shame as a series of automatic thoughts that have grown into a habit; they will cease to block our whole picture of who we are as magnificent people.

Why might this practice help us disentangle from the shame loop?

In the first part the **deeper breathing** activates the para-sympathetic nervous system which slows the heart rate, and puts the body in a resting state. The hand on the heart helps us feel safe and loved which activates the release of oxytocin in the brain. Recent studies have begun to investigate the role of oxytocin in various behaviours. They show that oxytocin, sometimes referred to as the 'love hormone', promotes trust and empathy and is the hormone of safety and trust, of 'calm and connect' and is an antidote to cortisol, the hormone of the stress response. Oxytocin is one the best resources we have to help us recover from toxic shame and when we activate it we feel loved and cherished.

The second part is called **centring**. Before we face the toxic shame we use mindfulness of the body to train the mind to focus our attention on our experience in the here and now without any reaction to it. Our shame memories are stored as body sensations without us even being aware of them. When we focus our attention on the body sensations we can retrain our mind to hold the experience without touching it or reacting to it. Mindfulness will help us not to respond to any experience or label it as positive or negative. The part of the brain that assesses danger is neutralized in the experience. We can let go of the experience and short-circuit the shame loop.

The third part **challenges our old memory patterns**. Most of the time when we are stuck in the shame loop we are re-experiencing old memories. These memories come from when we were very young. The shame is an early childhood response pattern. But we have no memory of what happened to us or why we responded as we did, but we still have the trigger that catapults us into the shame loop. This makes the experience seem to be related to something that is happening today. But of course it isn't and this part of the activity helps us with that old memory.

In the fourth part we employ the **power of observation**. When we step back and observe the experience of this moment and do so without criticism we are better able to see ourselves as something more than a ball of shame. In terms of the loving adult and the inner child, observation helps us to move out of the dark world of the depressed child and into the spaciousness of the loving parent.

In the fifth part we actively **restore the original compassion** we had when we were born. Studies have suggested that it takes 21 days to replace an old habit with a new habit. It's as if we can re-encode our bodies to reject the shame and embrace self-compassion. It's not so much that we get rid of the shame but more that we increase our awareness of the wider world and dissolve the shame in our greater awareness like a pinch of salt in a vast lake.

Healing the shame meditation activity

This will take five minutes. Doing it at least five times will help get into a rhythm that will break old habits and re-wire the brain. Read it or record it and listen to it.

1. Building Your internal resources.

Place your hand on top of your heart. Breathe gently and deeply into the centre of your heart. Breathe in all the love, safety, easiness, trust and acceptance you can. Once you've steadied your breathing, recall a moment of being with someone or something who loves you boundlessly. This is someone with whom you feel completely safe. It could be family but may also be a therapist, priest, good friend, a pet, your higher power, a teacher or someone who you trust to be on your side.

Let your safe feelings flow as you think about the safe and loved feelings with this person or pet. See if you can capture the sensations and feelings that come up. Let yourself float in the memory and relish the warmth and love in your body. Appreciate the trust and safe feelings that you experience. Hold on to this for at least 30 seconds. Then place your hands on your abdomen.

2. Centring

Be mindful of your breath going into your nose and down to your abdomen, and back up and out through your nose. Become aware of the difference in temperature when you breathe out. When you breathe in through the nose the breath is slightly cooler and when you breathe it out, it's slightly warmer. Practice settling into an open spacious awareness of what is happening in this moment. Don't respond, don't try to change it. Just allow and accept this moment without a story or a label. Just accept the way it is right at this moment. When you feel centred move on to the third part.

3. Accepting

Think now about the writing you did previously when feelings of shame came to you. Bring that memory of shame to this present moment and allow the awfulness of it to be felt. At the same time bring in compassion for yourself, acceptance of yourself and unconditional love. They will shelter the inner child and hold him so he's safe. In this part we become aware of the two separate parts of us – the shame-ridden child and the loving parent. If you can't find a loving parent within yourself bring to mind someone who you can trust without any doubt. Someone who you know loves you without strings and only wants the best for you. Feel their love coming inside you as a stream of light filling your whole body. Or bring in the love from your higher power and let it flood through you like a river.

4. Observation

Now step back from this experience and observe it without judging it. Step away from the shame that

you had and see it as just one experience out of many experiences that you have every day. As you step back you can see that that was how things were for you then, but now is different. You will be able to see the shame as only one part of a whole event.

5. Restoring

Now you have an awareness of where the shame sits in you, place your hands back on your heart and breathe more deeply. See yourself as a huge lake. What does the surface look like? If it is choppy, make it become still until it's like a mirror. When the choppy ripples have subsided you'll feel the deep peace of your being in the deep waters underneath the surface. Spend a moment in this awareness. The shame is no longer dominating you; it was one ripple on the surface and now it's gone. It does not define you, it is simply an embedded old memory. It's not a big deal and it doesn't have any power over you any longer.

This activity will take five minutes. The healing begins when it is done regularly. Regular practice will help to shift old memories and the associated toxic shame. You can do it in bed before you get up, in the bathroom at work, in the car when you arrive or before you leave, in fact anywhere you find you have five minutes to yourself. Update the shaming messages you hear until they've gone. This will take no more than three weeks.

AFFIRMATIONS

I'm aware of the shame inside me but I now realize it's an old message that has no part in my life today.

I throw out the feelings of shame; I have nothing to feel ashamed of.

I let my associated fear and anger flow away as I release the old beliefs that have outlived their usefulness. They are not relevant in my life today and never will be.

Today I focus on self-compassion, empathy and self-love.

Becoming Fully Responsible

The way to discover the power you never knew you had

W hen we suffer from depression we tend to believe that we are a lot more responsible for other people and situations than is good for us. Being overly responsible is needing to be in control. It is characterized by fear, force and a lack of trust that everything's going to turn out OK.

Some people truly believe that they are responsible for another person's happiness, especially someone whom they cherish. Everything may be going fine until the other person is not happy. Then we think it's our responsibility to put that right. Perhaps that's why we feel so depressed. Being overly responsible is born out of the need to have power over everything. We want things to happen our way because – basically – we're running scared and we don't trust things are going to work out OK. But things don't work out OK because we end up with physical and/ or emotional burn-out.

At the same time we *are* each completely responsible for our *own* life. We were born alone and we'll die alone; there is no safety net. No matter who we turn to for help, recovery from depression is down to us. Others can guide us and make suggestions but they can't do the work for us. As adults we are 100% responsible for *ourselves*. But, if we're depressed we can't see this.

This was a tough lesson for me to learn and, to a certain extent, still is. Being responsible for myself, not being responsible for anyone else and not looking to anyone else to fix me are traits I have to work on daily. However, I'm grateful for the opportunity because I've grown up. Life-long patterns that came from being raised by an alcoholic mother, who told me I was responsible for ruining her life, were hard to change. This is the work I had to focus on to get a reality check. Was I really *not* responsible for other people's feelings? It took me a while truly to believe it. But I have (more or less) and now I'm living a depression-free life. My biggest problem is *not to feel guilty* when I stand up for myself and put my needs first. That still comes up each time I put myself first but I'm working on it.

What stops us from being fully responsible for ourselves? *Trying to live other people's lives!* It's a trap. We think we're 'helping' but in fact we're making ourselves depressed by getting involved in other people's lives trying to 'fix and rescue' them. We anticipate other people's needs, then feel angry when they don't do what we want them to do. We try to please others instead of ourselves. We find it easier to express anger about things done to others rather than things done to us. We feel guilty when someone tries to help us. We feel worthless and empty if we don't have someone to help. We blame others for the distress we feel. We believe other people are making us depressed.

The victim/persecutor see-saw

A simple analogy can help to demonstrate what happens to us when we don't take responsibility for ourselves, instead preferring to be caught up in other people lives. It's called the 'victim/persecutor see-saw'. At one end we have the persecutor and, at the other, the victim. We continually see-saw from one type of thinking to the other.

Victim thinking

When we're depressed we see ourselves as victims. We are victims of society because we can't get where we want to be, of our childhood because of the way we were raised, of our friends abandoning us, getting a raw deal from our workplace, others' behaviour in our relationships, and so on. We compare ourselves with others and generally come bottom of the pile. Other people seem to have so much going for them, get good luck, land on their feet, never have anything to worry about and have people giving them a break. We the victims, on the other hand, see ourselves having bad luck, being in the wrong place at the wrong time, dealing with insurmountable stress and having unavoidable pressures placed on us. We become locked into a lifetime of 'victim thinking' and it doesn't make us happy. In fact it makes us depressed!

Persecutor thinking

Many of us have the capacity to turn into persecutors when we've had enough of being 'victimized' by others. We may end up saying things like: *you always do that to me*; *you should think before you speak to me like that*; *you never help me when I need it*; *I'm always doing things for you and you never thank me*. We're the worm that turned and we may be so surprised at our success in making others do what we want that we step into this role more often!

Persecutors are the bullies of life. We may not think of ourselves in this way but all of us have the capacity to become one, especially when we're depressed. Acting as the persecutor is a defence mechanism, a way to run from our pain. We're hurting so much that all we can do is lash out like a wounded animal. We think if we don't dominate others then they will dominate us, which will push the see-saw back the other way so we become the victim again and that terrifies us. This see-saw thinking can dominate our whole lives and we may not even know it.

The victim/persecutor trap

When we're trapped in victim/persecutor thinking, we truly believe that others are responsible for us. This thinking is usually established in childhood and it comes as a revelation to many of us when we learn about it for the first time. Even though we can rationalize that the victim is often an unwilling and unhappy participant, the persecutor is also a victim because they too feel trapped. When we're into 'victim-thinking' mode we can lock ourselves into believing others should feel sorry for us or 'save' us, and thus we unwittingly step into a helpless, childlike role. When we're into the 'persecutor-thinking' mode we trap ourselves into believing that we have to fight our way out of a bad situation because we've been harmed, judged or bad-mouthed and it's up to us to *sort it out!* We didn't mean to get trapped but sometimes, it's all we've ever known.

Let's get a clarification in here: this isn't about someone who was in the wrong place at the wrong time and has had a crime committed against them like someone who's been mugged. This is about repeated 'victim-thinking' patterns that trap people into a state of mind that perpetuates victimhood, the sort of thinking that can lead us to believe there are only two roles in life – those who get what they want and those who don't.

The real trap bites when someone reaches out with a hand of love and support and we can't accept it. The victim in us secretly doesn't want to change because being the victim is comfortable: it's what we know. Others try to help us but when we they tell us how beautiful, powerful, intelligent and lovable we are, we can't take it on board. We can't believe they are telling the truth. We think they are saying these things to try and get us to do something, feel better or get out of their way. We think they are lying or have ulterior motives. They get angry because we don't respond how they want us to respond and this makes us feel even more victimized. We're caught up in others' lives and find it hard to map out our own edges. Who is responsible for whom?

For a long time I thought that I could only be happy if I was in a relationship. I couldn't see myself being happy without one. It was as if I didn't exist outside of a relationship. I was like an 'add-on' to someone else's life. Nothing made sense without a relationship. I had no 'me' – I had no idea who Alex was. I needed a relationship to make me feel whole. The problem was I needed it to be run on my terms because I was trying to shore up my crumbling self-esteem. I was controlling, manipulative, depressed and I really, really believed that it was the other person's responsibility *to make me happy.* Having done much recovery work, I can look back and see how much pain I was running from and how I was desperately hoping someone else could fix me.

Many of us have become victims because we consistently give more than we receive and try to anticipate what others need, then get angry when no one gives back to us. And we genuinely feel guilty when someone does give to us so it's hard to climb out of the trap. We're so focused on what others want *and what they want us to be* that if we're not wanted, we feel rejection and dismay.

Getting off the see-saw

If I were to tell you that this trap is an illusion, would you believe me? Yes it's true. What is missing are the alternatives. When we're depressed we tend to see life as black or white. Getting off the see-saw means seeing the other shades and a whole spectrum of colour in between. It is possible to get off the see-saw and be neither the victim nor persecutor. We can become more than this thinking. Just because life has dealt us a series of blows and we've felt more pain than we thought possible, it doesn't mean it's going to be like this for ever. But we need to give ourselves time, and love. We need to employ our loving parent and ask for help from our higher power. Once we begin to put changes in place, life opens up for us. Each of us has the potential to enjoy a worthwhile and joyous life no matter where we've come from.

The difference between being over-responsible for others and taking responsibility for ourselves

To step off the see-saw we must identify how we take responsibility for other people. We think we're being selfless but the real definition of that word is self-less. We are not taking care of the self; in fact we make our self-worth less than it is. When we do this we are abdicating responsibility for ourselves by preferring to put others' needs above our own.

Here is a comparison between being over-responsible for others and taking responsibility for ourselves:

Being over-responsible for others	Taking responsibility for ourselves
• feeling responsible for others' choices • and others' feelings • assuming we know what others are thinking • taking the blame for everything going wrong • but not the credit when it goes right • giving advice when it's not asked for • thinking we know what's right for others • doing things that are not helpful to us • blaming others when our life goes belly-up • getting angry when people don't do what we want • abandoning our lives to make way for someone else's life • over-committing to others • saying yes when we mean no We ask questions or make statements like: • 'Do you still love me?' • 'I'm nothing without you' • 'After all I do for you …' • 'You always …' • 'You never …' • 'You'll never leave me will you?'	• accepting that no one else puts thoughts in our head; seems silly but amazing when we think about it … no one else can make us think about things we don't want to think about • accepting that we choose our life direction and knowing we can't blame others for how it turns out • being our real selves with other people and feeling good about it • understanding we are our own best guide and that we don't look to other people to make us feel good • knowing that no matter what we feel, negative or positive, no one 'made' us feel that way and we are 100% responsible • believing that, no matter what's happened in the past, no one else is responsible for us now • accepting the consequences of all our actions • not accepting any responsibility for others (except our children) • appreciating we are 100% responsible for our own personal growth, emotional stability, physical health and self-esteem • being honest about our talents and skills

This over-responsible behaviour is often characterized by an intense anxiety around relationships. We find ourselves monitoring the dynamics between us and others and dedicating ourselves to what others need. We often have strong ideas of how things 'should' be and can be overly helpful in trying to fix things, all in a desperate quest to quell our own anxiety. This behaviour can lead us into the 'trap' of the victim – and we're back on the see-saw. Then we can blame the 'other' for our depression. It's hard to see our part when we're stuck because we truly believe we are being kind and selfless.

Let's go through some steps to begin to redress the balance. The starting point is to take good care of ourselves.

Taking good care

Let's acknowledge what 'taking good care' is not. It isn't putting our own needs above everyone else's at their expense. For example, if I want a new wardrobe and I spend the family housekeeping on getting it, leaving no money for groceries, and say 'I'm just taking care of myself' – it won't wash. Turning up at my parents' home for a fortnight's holiday without being invited because I'm 'taking care of my needs' doesn't cut it. This isn't about greed, manipulation or imposing what *I want* on anyone else.

Taking good care is a new way of thinking. It is as follows:

> I am responsible for me. I am responsible for meeting my own needs, for taking care of my own spiritual path, taking care of my body, eating healthily, financing my life, ensuring my emotional needs are taken care of (by getting the right help if necessary) and for living my own life. I am responsible for choosing who I give to or take from, setting life goals and sticking to them or changing course if I choose to. Responsibility for the outcome of my life lies at my door and will be the result of what I think, feel and how I behave. I am responsible for choosing who I love and whose love I choose to receive. I'm responsible for the compromises

I make to get my needs met. I value the choices I've made and I will accept the consequences of the choices that haven't worked out so well. I will make decisions that will increase my self-worth and if they don't I will accept responsibility for this.

I will not allow others to abuse me, because I have rights and it's my responsibility to assert these rights. I value my rights and the decisions I make around them. However, these are my rights and I don't have to force them on others. I respect others' rights and that their feelings and decisions are different to mine. I won't impose my decisions on others and expect others not to impose their decisions on me. Finally, I will be mindful of how my decisions affect those people with whom I have relationships.

Taking good care isn't selfish, it's self-responsible. It's meeting our needs. We can't meet anyone else's needs until we can fulfil our own. Learning to meet our needs and be responsible for the outcome is the path to freedom and new choices. We can learn to take care of our needs very quickly. We know what we need and we have the internal resources to seek ways of getting them fulfilled.

The healing begins when we begin self-care. This is the alternative to accepting responsibility for others. Self-care is learning what we need to feel good and a simple way is to ask ourselves: what do I need to take care of myself? We turn to our higher power, we write the question in our journal and we trust our loving parent. We need to dig deep and listen for the answers. There's a saying that goes:

We ask with prayer and we listen to the answer with meditation

We have to challenge the limitations of our thinking when we punish ourselves for having needs. All of us are human and humans have needs. When we think that others have deserted us we can turn that thought around and notice that we have

113

deserted ourselves. Once we do that we can take positive action.

There is another lovely saying:

Everything will come to you at the right time

And it's true. My experience is that I've always got what I needed at the right time. It may not have been what I *wanted* but it was what I needed. It helped me change and grow and flourish.

Developing gentleness and compassion

Gentleness and compassion is at the heart of taking good care of yourself. No one needs it more than those of us who've suffered from depression. Listening to your inner child and taking his needs seriously is compassion at its best. When you're pole-axed with depression perhaps all you need is a safe place to hide. Taking yourself to bed, wrapping up in a blanket and sipping a hot drink is gentleness at its best. We are humans trying to do our best and somehow we got lost. Feeling the warmth of your loving parent and lighting a candle for a soothing bath is a good way of slowing down. Giving yourself a treat or a fun day out is kind and caring. We can start with small things like taking care of ourselves with consideration rather than like a critical parent.

Trust is the way out

Many people have been victimized at some stage in their lives; perhaps this has happened to you. Often this trait is seeded in childhood. Victim thinking may have caused a lot of harm and driven us into a corner. However, once we realize this, we have an obligation to ourselves to turn this around 180 degrees.

We don't have to continue to feel like a victim. By understanding that feeling like a victim is *only a thought* we have the starting point that can help us to move out of this unhelpful thinking.

It's only a thought!

You may have to go on trust alone until you've worked through the activities at the end of this step and begin to feel the difference when you take full responsibility for your life and claim your own power. I had to get on my knees, every day, sometimes every hour, to get through this. I begged for help to take away the blackness I was left with after beating myself up. Time after time I thought I'd done the wrong thing, talked out of turn, let everyone down, failed my goals, behaved in a bad way, made others ashamed of me and so on. It turns out, 99% of what I experienced was a fantasy that I was locked – yes, *locked* – into. It was all in my head and yet I thought it was really happening. That is the craziness of the victim/persecutor thinking. It almost destroyed me and I didn't realize I had the power to change it until it was almost too late. However, I did, and here I am writing about it. Those hours on knees begging for help and trusting in my higher power got me through. The activities that follow are also part of the work I did to realign my thinking.

ACTIVITIES

Here are three activities which can help you to discover:

1. When you take on responsibility for others.
2. Learning to say yes and no.
3. How to reduce your reactive responses.

Activity 1: When we take on responsibility for others.

Write down in detail everything you consider as your responsibility. Do this for your work, your marriage/relationship, the raising of your children, your interactions with siblings, friends and parents. Make a clear and detailed list of what you believe to be your responsibilities in these areas. Next to your responsibilities, outline what you believe to be other people's responsibilities in the same areas. If you share some responsibilities, roughly mark out what percentage of the responsibility is yours. And then mark out the percentage responsibility of others.

For example, if you have shared responsibilities in your job, work out what is yours – the bit that was set at the beginning of the job when the role was given to you. You may be surprised at how much extra responsibility you have taken on without questioning it. Once you've done this, try to understand exactly what you hoped to gain by taking on this extra responsibility. It may be that you were hoping your boss would notice how much extra you've been prepared to take on. In the role of the fixer, our extra responsibilities rarely get acknowledged or even noticed!

Now you've identified areas where you take on too much responsibility, become more aware in everyday life how you act out that role. When you find yourself being over-responsible, stop, step back and notice your mood. Do you feel annoyed that you've done something nice for someone and they've taken no notice? Or do you feel hurt that they haven't thanked you? Have you ignored your own needs at the same time?

Making changes might be frightening to begin with. Will the other person still like me? Will old friends still speak to me if I stop putting them first? Will my parents chastise me for not being good enough? It takes some personal courage to step out of type. But it's what will move you away from depression.

Stop making assumptions. It's important to realize that when we're depressed we do a lot of assuming about what others think. We believe we can mind-read! And we adjust our actions to avert those thoughts we think others have. Of course all of this is supposition. It's an old habit and hard to break but it's essential to regain our self-confidence. So as you make a decision NOT to fix someone else, frame the thoughts you think another person is going to have about you.

These thoughts are actually your thoughts.

They are what you would think if you were on the receiving end of you. So now you have to replace those assumptions with some positive thoughts.

For example, if you were asked to look after your friend's child for the day and you didn't want to, you could say 'No I'm sorry I'm unable to help out.' But you may hesitate and suppose that your friend would think you were unkind. That thought *your friend would think you were unkind* is not the friend's thought; that's your thought. That's you telling yourself that it would be unkind *not* to help your friend. So you might say 'yes' because you didn't want your friend to think badly of you. However, that whole dialogue has taken place without the friend even knowing about it. That's where we mess with our own heads and end up feeling resentful for doing something we didn't want to do.

Another example is if you try to help your girlfriend who's drinking too much. You *know* what's right for her and that's to stop drinking all together. You haven't asked her but you know you're right. You search carefully about how to get her to stop drinking, contact the doctor or Alcoholics Anonymous or book her into rehab (at your expense) and feel fantastic when she dries out. However, a few weeks down the line she's fallen off the wagon and is right back where she started, happily drunk. You on the other hand are outraged. After all you've done, and paid for, for her, she has the audacity to throw it back in your face and start drinking again!

Two examples that go from the sublime to the ridiculous. All of our own doing. So how do we change it?

Activity 2: Learning to say yes and no

Setting clear personal boundaries is the key to helping our relationships become mutually respectful. The more boundaries we set the more our self-worth increases. Setting boundaries can be firm but also gentle. We don't need to alienate others but do need to set limits for acceptable behaviour with those around us.

When I began this work I didn't have a clue what my boundaries were. I wobbled all over the place trying to figure them out. Essentially I didn't know myself – so how the hell could I know my boundaries? This activity helped me to clarify when I said 'yes' when I didn't want to, and how I could learn to say 'no' without feeling ashamed.

How we say yes when we don't want to

1. Start by making a decision to put yourself first for the next two weeks.

2. Make a note of all the things you need to do to tick the 'my responsibilities' list from activity one.
3. Next make a list of all the things you would like to do with the time (and resources) you have left that will nourish you. This might be arranging some childcare so you can go out with friends, attend three yoga classes a week, cook up your favourite foods, play football in the park, spend every moment beautifying yourself, dig over the garden, spend time on your relationship, or anything else.
4. Choose the top three priorities and write them on a piece of paper and stick it where you can see it.
5. For the next two weeks make a note of how many times you agree to do something which isn't on your priority list.

You will be surprised at how many times you said 'yes' to something that wasn't on your list. It's hard to change a lifetime's habit but then it's harder being depressed for a long time. The thing to remember is that a happier you is better for everyone else around you.

Here's how to say no

1. Make a note of all the things you don't want to do over the next two weeks. These could be a commitment you want to give up, an appointment you don't want to keep or a meal you don't want to eat. Imagine there would be no negative consequences if you said no to any of these things.
2. Prioritize them so you get to your top three and write them on a piece of paper, sticking it somewhere you can see it.
3. Start with the smallest no and practise that until you feel comfortable about moving on to the bigger ones.

The biggest hurdle you will face is to overcome guilt. Instead of racking your head with guilt, see it as your first step towards a new life. Guilt will happen but it doesn't mean you have to act on it. You can explain to others that you are taking better care of yourself and consequently you've had to change your priorities. Anyone worth their salt is going to respect this change and be supportive. You can overcome any remaining guilt through mindful meditation and radical acceptance – tools which are at the end of this step.

Healing our victim/perpetrator with mindfulness

We begin to abandon the victim/perpetrator role by becoming more honest with ourselves. We become an observer of our behaviour and, if we think about people whom we have uncomfortable relationships with, we can ask ourselves which role we are playing. We don't need to mend it; we only need to become aware of it. Becoming aware of our behaviour is mindfulness at its best. We notice what is happening rather than reacting to it and we watch how we're about to get hooked back in. Being mindful of our behaviour is the most powerful way to stop us walking blindly into these roles.

When we practise being mindful in difficult relationships, we don't need to judge anyone else's behaviour. What we need to do is become accountable for our own thoughts and feelings and the behaviours that keep us stuck in these roles. If we take care of ourselves and our feelings all our problems are resolved. If we expect others to take care of their feelings and problems, we stop trying to fix them. It doesn't take long to step off the see-saw and see that we don't need to try and sort other people's lives out. In our mind they become responsible for themselves (even though they already were) which means that our load is lightened.

When we suffer from depression we tend to worry about what other people think of us or we assume that other people think badly of us. The truth is what other people think of us is none of our business. Just as what we think of other people is none of their business. Our business is to change ourselves so that we feel good about ourselves; that is our business.

Another thing we do is to beat ourselves up for making a mistake. But consider this, if a child you loved dearly made a simple mistake in something he said or did, would you beat him up? No! You would ruffle his hair and tell him it was OK and that he will learn from his mistake. That's what you have to do for you.

Activity 3: How to reduce your reactive responses

This is an activity to get you thinking how you react – or over-react – to others. When we over-react we are coming from a victim viewpoint. We think we're at the mercy of others. But we're not, unless we've given them permission. We can, instead, make a conscious decision to stop feeling at the mercy of others because we're not helpless and we always have a choice.

Open your journal and write down the answers to these questions. Take your time. It can be done over days or weeks and if you redo the exercise at a later date you may have different perspectives. These questions may seem tough but we have to be a little tough from time to time. Being gentle all the time won't work. We need to be objective about our behaviour and how it's getting us into trouble. We have to change certain behaviour because it's harming us. These questions are designed to get you thinking about which role you take on; they are exploratory and not definitive.

Answer them gently and in the spirit of needing understanding, not to self-criticize. They will help you feel more in control of your responses to difficult scenarios.

- Who do I want to be responsible for me?
- What do I want them to do for me or give me?
- How does my body respond when I look to someone to rescue me?
- What statements do I use that make me behave like a victim?
- What does it feel like to be at the mercy of another's response?
- How can I learn to handle saying no to another person?
- What beliefs do I have about my being allowed to say no?

- What examples can I think of when I'm stuck on the see-saw?
- Do I identify more with the victim or perpetrator?
- What role am I in when I get angry?
- How can I increase caring for myself?
- How do I deal with conflict?

Here's a list of things I can consider to handle situations better:

- How can I be more responsible for my emotions?
- How can I find the courage to be more honest with safe people?
- How do I reject others?
- Have I placed unrealistic expectations on others?
- Have I been inappropriately angry with others?
- How can I use that energy to propel me out of depression?
- Am I ready to be more vulnerable with others?

Turn 'accept responsibility' into 'becoming response-able'

If someone has carried out an act that is abusive towards us, who is responsible for the pain that it causes? Consider this: the same abusive act can be experienced by several people and they will all have a different response. Some people might think 'Well it wasn't personal to me.' Others might think 'What did I do to deserve that?' Everyone has a different indicator of pain in the same situation. We are responsible for the level of pain and the control button that makes it go up or down. Those of us who suffer from depression will know that our pain switch varies but we often struggle to keep it on low, which would indicate that our ability to respond well to the situation is also low.

This happens when we 'react' to a situation instead of responding to it. Reactions are generally based way back in childhood patterns of behaviour – but responses can be made today. Being response-able is when we think before we feel, try to rationalize a situation and don't jump in with a knee-jerk reaction. We don't assume everything is our fault. We apportion responsibility appropriately. For example if someone shouted at me, instead of feeling like a worm, I could step back and ask myself why they shouted. I could rationalize the behaviour as unnecessary – unless it was vital because of an emergency situation – and take a view on how I wanted to respond. This is taking response-ability.

The more we do this the more we reduce our reactive responses because we calm down the response stimulus. This makes us free to be more *responsive*, which then helps us have more control and choices about how we wish to behave in other people's company. As a result our self-worth increases, which strengthens our ability to stay strong, no matter what others say to us or about us. Our *reactions* no longer drag us into the den of iniquity: self-loathing, self-pity and ultimately depression. We respond with the head of an adult rather than the battered emotions of a child. We don't let others walk over us because we have new strength and power.

Practising this can help us to break old patterns when others try to drag us back into destructive behaviour. Reacting to others gives them fire to play with – and we are the ones who end up getting burned. If we respond rather than react, we retain our power. For example if someone pointed their finger at me and accused me of not being a nice person, my response is not to defend myself but to say something like 'an interesting point of view'. The moment I argue back I continue a cycle of attack/retreat/defence. Apologizing, arguing or explaining my standpoint only gives the other person permission to continue to react. But by using a phrase like 'I'll take that away and think about it' we are responding politely and respectfully but at the same time, setting our boundaries.

One very simple way of moving from a *responsibility* standpoint to having response-ability is to change your vocabulary. Here are a few examples:

Instead of saying	Say
I'll never be able to stand up to them.	I haven't yet stood up to them but I'm working towards it.
I'll never get the job I want.	I haven't got the job I want yet but I'm two positions away from my ideal job.
I can't.	I choose not to.
I mustn't.	I won't at the moment.
I'll never.	Not right now.
I'll always.	I am for now but it won't be for ever.

You can see that the first set of statements are limiting and closed, with no way forward. The second set of statements are open, and allow for change, growth and flexibility. By taking a moment before clicking into that knee-jerk reaction, we are better able to get a rational take on a situation and be response-able.

Stepping off the see-saw helps us to become more self-aware, grow up emotionally and beat depression faster. Once we have gained the awareness of our behaviour and changed from taking responsibility to being response-able, the game of see-saw is over!

Visualization

This visualization is to help us move away from the victim/persecutor thinking and anchor ourselves in our own conscious awareness. It includes an anchoring technique based on a Neuro-Linguistic Programming (NLP) tool. Remember the dots mean a pause. It lasts 10 minutes and is for anyone who struggles in a relationship and wants to find their own strength. It's best to record it into a device you can listen to in safety and comfort. Our own voice is usually the best voice to listen to because it speaks directly to the unconscious part of us.

Settle down in a comfortable chair sitting upright with your feet on the floor. Make sure you are in a room where you can't be disturbed. . . . Now bring your attention to your breath . . . . and feel the rise and fall of the abdomen as your breath moves in and out. Sit here

for a moment and let your breath be your guide . . . . As
you breathe in and out . . . . you may notice your mind
is wandering off in thoughts . . . . or that you experience
physical sensations in your body . . . . Simply escort
your mind back to the breath and feel the breath going
in . . . . and out . . . . and in . . . . and out . . . . now bring
your attention into your body . . . . and become aware
of the physical sensations in your body . . . . especially
the centre of your body . . . . as if a piece of rope was
connecting you from the sky to the earth . . . . and
running all the way through your body . . . . from
the sky down into your head . . . . and neck . . . . and
back . . . . and abdomen . . . . and bottom . . . . and
pulling tight so you have to sit up straight . . . . and
bring your attention back to your breath . . . . moving in
through the nose and out through the mouth . . . . Now
imagine you are in the middle of the see-saw . . . . and
at each end are the victim . . . . and persecutor . . . . and
you are standing in the middle of this see-saw . . . . and
bring your awareness back to your breath . . . . going
in . . . . and going out . . . . and as you stand strong in
the middle of the see-saw . . . . you can see the roles
being played out on each end of the see-saw . . . . and
these roles are being played out by you and another
person . . . . but at this point you are not affected by
what is being played out . . . . you are simply observing
what is going on . . . . whilst you pay attention to
your breath . . . . coming in and your breath going
out . . . . trying not to judge or criticize what is going on
on the see-saw . . . . it is simply your job to be aware of
it . . . . As you stand strong in the middle of the see-saw
you become still and calm . . . . there is no movement
no thought and no reaction . . . . you simply accept
the roles being played out on the see-saw . . . . while
you stand completely still in the middle . . . . And if
you take a look under the see-saw you will see that
the bottom of the rope has gone through the see-saw

and turned into a steel rope.... and is embedded in a steel core which in turn is entrenched into the earth.... that rope is holding you in place.... strong and powerful.... and in control.... You are the master of your own destiny.... you no longer need others to define you.... Feel the power inside you .... and feel the release of any need to meet other people's demands.... Feel the strength that brings to you.... and now bring your left thumb and your left index finger together and press them hard.... while you feel this powerful energy inside you.... and stay with this feeling for as long as you want to allow it to feed you and nourish you and love you.... With your finger and thumb pressing together and anchoring this feeling.... you can come back any time.... to this special, powerful place.

Repeat this visualization once a day for at least seven days. Once you've established the 'anchor' you can use this technique to make a big difference to your ability to deal with people. Instead of hoping you will feel response-able when you next need to express yourself, just bring together your index finger and thumb which will drop your anchor and bring you to the same feeling you had in the visualization.

AFFIRMATIONS

No one can think for me, feel for me or give meaning to my life except me.

I will learn to pause before I respond to another. I no longer need to play the old games of knee-jerk reactions. I won't worry about what others think of me.

Managing my over-reactions can help me to rebalance and stop me from bouncing from high to low and back to high again.

*When I respond instead of react I am able to respond
with dignity and grace.*

*I will feel comfortable with not knowing
and that I have limited control over life.
I cannot control outputs, only inputs.*

*No one can experience my life for me.
My journey is unique to me.*

Mind over Matter

Stopping the madness of mind racing

O ne thing we all do when we're depressed – we think. But it's not just any old thinking; this is real hard-core thinking. And it's not just real hard-core thinking but we do it at frightening speed. It's called 'mind racing' and it's what happens when we let our mind run free. Mind racing is constantly playing back different scenarios with different outcomes of what could have been or might be. It's a major energy drain but we do it without realizing it. It keeps us from being in the present moment and acts as a shield from our depression. If we were driving during a bout of mind racing we could drive a hundred miles without necessarily remembering how we got there. That's what depressive thinking does: takes you out of reality and into an unreal world.

The medics call it rumination

That medical profession actually has a word for this type of thinking. It's called rumination. Rumination is when someone goes over and over and over negative thoughts. It's actually a compulsive focused attention on our distress, its possible causes and consequences. When we are in the middle of full-blown mind racing, *we only see problems*. Once we get into this very negative form of thinking it interferes with our ability to see any light at the end of the tunnel.

Research shows that our tendency to try and think our way out of the depression is harmful and could make us more depressed. Over-thinking is also linked to negative behaviour like self-harming, binge eating and drinking, and general anxiety. We try to *think* our way *out of* our depression but we're actually driving ourselves *further into* its clutches. Mind racing can be experienced as a background 'white noise' and can take over a person's ability to be aware of what going on. Mind racing also seems to be very repetitive and overwhelming, which results in losing track of time.

Generally, mind racing is when the mind brings up random thoughts and memories and switches between them very quickly; we have no control over it. Usually the thoughts are focused on one or two things but at the same time they pop out randomly. If we suffer from mind racing we can't easily slow down these thought patterns and it can begin to affect our health. Mind racing can disrupt sleep patterns which pushes up stress levels. It also keeps us in a crisis by going over and over imagined threats. Somehow, and this is the crazy part, we think it's doing us good. We imagine the worst possible scenario so that if we ever have to face it for real, we'll be ready!

Here's a quick quiz to see if you suffer from a racing mind:

1. Do you find yourself automatically thinking about problems when you're doing things that allow your mind to be on idle, like cleaning, driving or trying to fall asleep?
2. Do you find meditation tricky because thoughts bombard you?
3. Would others suggest that you love drama and that if you don't have one you either create one or get in the middle of someone else's?
4. Do you ever wake up in the middle of the night and can't get back to sleep because you're thinking so much?
5. Are you a glass half-empty kind of person thinking that things won't work out rather than that things will work out?

6. When you think about things in your life that upset you, do you feel overwhelmed, stressed and depressed, and then focus on those feelings too?
7. When you're dealing with a conflict with another person, do you find yourself working into a fury but feel like you can't do anything about it and then feel worse?
8. If you talk with your friends about a situation that makes you angry, upset or stressed, do you prefer to have your friends see it your from your side and then get upset if they don't?

If you've answered yes to four or more of these questions then you may well suffer from mind racing.

Negative default position

There is an added disadvantage for anyone who has previously suffered from a deep depression. Depression makes a connection in the brain between mind racing and a sad mood. It's like a line drawn in the sand and any normal sadness can take us back behind that line in the sand – our default position – without us even trying. Studies have shown this to be the case and it helps us to understand why, when we feel sad, we give up on ourselves so easily.

For some of us no matter how well we are doing when we trip up we don't seem to go just one step back; we seem to slide all the way down the bottom – like sliding down the snake of the snakes and ladders board back to the starting point. Sometimes it seems we just can't get ourselves out of the depression no matter what we do. This can add to our feeling of hopelessness and helplessness.

So what happens?

Mind racing is a psychic disease (or dis-ease.) It's almost an epidemic because everyone does it and it seems unstoppable. But it works in the same way for everyone. This is mind racing's method of operation.

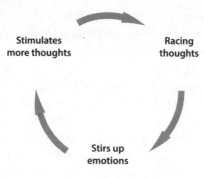

Stimulates
more thoughts

Racing
thoughts

Stirs up
emotions

The mind racing loop

As the mind races away in the brain, it goes over and over something: we're no good, or nothing good will ever happen to us, or we're worthless and useless. What happens is that thought stimulates emotions like fear, anxiety, frustration, anger and panic. Those emotions then get played out and not in a good way. Emotions are essentially the body's way of reacting to the mind. For example, if we tell ourselves that we're in trouble, our bodies will go into the 'fight or flight' mode which sets up fear and anxiety. If we tell ourselves that we're totally useless, this feels punishing and we feel the negative energy in our chest or abdomen. Of course we don't intend to do this but we do it unconsciously. The more unconscious this process, the more it becomes apparent in the body and if this happens day in, day out, it's no wonder we feel beaten!

On its own, mind racing could cause us to get depressed. If we did nothing else except learn how to master the mind, this could be the only thing we need to help us to beat depression fast. Sometimes the answers to the most complex problems are actually simple, and this is one of them. Generally speaking anyone who suffers from depression suffers from mind racing. This type of mind is like a thousand dominos all set up; the mind pushes the first domino and the whole row falls down. Except they keep falling and never stop. Each thought creates an emotion until we're a series of unconscious reactions keeping us in this loop of madness. And we wonder why we are so depressed!

A reality check

When we're depressed we work under the assumption that incessant thinking is imperative to our well-being. But it isn't. Let's have a think about this!

When we think, or ruminate, we think about the same thing over and over again. This thinking is like a paralysis and prevents us from moving forwards. But what are we thinking about? We think about three things.

1. **The past.** When we think about the past we reactivate an old memory and attach regret or remorse to it. Regret because we've lost something we wish we still had or remorse for something we wish hadn't happened. But that is madness because the past will never be in our life today; it can't, it's impossible.

2. **The future.** We project a fantasy onto what we think may come true. This projection may be good, in which case we're attaching ourselves to something that we can't have now which causes frustration or it may be bad so we attach ourselves to a whole heap of fear based on a fantasy which may or may not come true. Again this is madness because when the future arrives, it becomes now.

3. **How we feel about ourselves in this moment.** If we suffer from depression then the chances are those thoughts are condemning and not at all helpful. 'You're useless, worthless and can't do anything right' is the kind of thing we think. This thinking triggers fear and self-hate which stirs up more thinking.

But all three types of thought can't be resolved by more thinking. They can't be resolved at all. But what can be resolved is to stop thinking altogether.

When I first tried to stop thinking, I thought it was going to take years of practice and great discipline. At first it did. My mind was crammed with racing thoughts like a bucket full of live eels squirming all over each other with nowhere to go. I thought I had to try harder and forced myself to be more disciplined.

But it didn't work. I just thought harder! I now realize that I was simply trying too hard and *I didn't need to try at all*. In fact 'trying' was the block to my happiness. I realized that there was nothing to try for and by *trying* to be more peaceful, it was having the opposite effect. Thinking about how I could be more peaceful next week was the antithesis of what I was trying to achieve, peace – now. Once I stopped spending time and energy trying to *think* my way out of my problems and accepted that I would always have problems, I found the peace I was desperately seeking. This was the first step to beating depression. I'd spent so long trying to 'sort out my life'; I'd forgotten how to *be* in my life. I finally realized that:

It was only a thought.

How to stop thinking

Asking ourselves how to stop thinking may seem like an extraordinary request. However we are on an extraordinary journey. Anyone who has suffered from the devastation of depression knows all too well what it's like to exist on the fringe of society. When we are in the depths of suffering it seems as though we are stationary and life moves on in front of us – over there! We need to take extraordinary steps if we want to beat depression *fast*. Forget convention, put aside scepticism and just try this step which, if taken seriously, can reframe the rest of your life. The art of no thought has been pursued for thousands of years by masters searching for enlightenment. We don't concern ourselves too much with the rationale of this step. All we need to know is that it works and can help us beat depression fast.

Read (or record and listen to) this whenever you want some peace from your frantic mind:

> We stop thinking by stopping thinking. At the moment that sounds easy but it is the hardest thing in the world until we simply stop thinking about it. How do we do that? Well the first thing to do is to recognize how much we are thinking. If we think about our minds

and our thoughts we can see the brain spinning like a roundabout. It moves so quickly we can't see each thought because it spins like a whirling dervish. Just take a few moments to watch the thoughts spinning around in your brain.

As you spend some time watching this roundabout of thoughts whizzing around in your brain you are beginning to step back from mind racing.... Get a bit of distance between you and it. Imagine you're stepping off the roundabout and watching it.... As you do this you disconnect your mind from your emotion. The negative messages stop by simply watching the mind at work 'up there' on the roundabout.

Don't try to understand the logic behind this because you start thinking again. Simply listen to these words slowly and carefully and this will help you get some distance from the mind. It's important not to try to stop thinking because that is the judgement which comes from thinking. Learning not to think isn't something you need to work hard at it's more like a light being switched on. There's nothing more to it than that. If you are thinking about it – just don't think. There is nothing to think about.

Whilst you're reading this passage you may be thinking this is nonsense but that's the thinker at work. Every time you hear the thinker at work, step back and watch the roundabout spinning.... up there.

Thinking and practising not thinking don't go together because you can't do both at the same time. While you're reading (or listening to) these words slowly and clearly, stop for a split-second in between each sentence and find the space before you read the next sentence. As you find a space between each sentence bring your awareness into that space. This awareness is your still presence.... If a thought arises.... just watch it.... don't be drawn into it.

When you catch yourself thinking you are free of

thinking. Catching yourself thinking puts some space in between you and your thoughts. If you couldn't catch yourself thinking you couldn't see that you've been thinking. If you feel frustrated at these words it's because your mind has told you you've failed. But you are not your mind and you haven't failed, you have just thought you've failed. If you suffer from depression it's because you believe everything your mind thinks. But you are not your mind, you are the space under the thoughts of your mind.

Can you feel the space in between each sentence? It's possible to think you've failed yet also feel the space between you and your mind. If you become very still you will find that space is like a sacred emptiness in the very centre of you. But don't think about it because the mind cannot process it. It's a different sense like a sixth sense, an awareness or even an awakening. Allow this moment to be as it is . . . . this will bring you back into the still place.

One of the questions we ask ourselves is 'What's wrong with me, why am I so depressed?' But that's our mind asking that question, it's not us. When we listen to our racing minds we are re-engaged in the dis-ease of our incessant thoughts. So, when we stop thinking we stop the questions. There is no need to answer these questions because there's no answer and there's no question.

Simply watch the thoughts spinning around and step away from them, coming into the sacred space that's left. You may think this is total nonsense but then you're back in your thoughts. But if you continue this practice of no thinking you will reverse the mind-racing loop and it will slow down. Become aware of your breathing instead of your thoughts. Become aware of the place that has no thoughts.

If you beat yourself up because you can't not think, that's the thinker's way of hooking you back in . . . . by stirring up the emotions and getting you back on the thinking loop. So the answer is to not think. In between each sentence find a space of no thought. As you read and re-read these words you will be able to stretch that split-second of no thought to a whole second and then two and then three. Once you hit three seconds you will touch the bliss that lies waiting for you underneath the thoughts. This is your true happiness, your true calling . . . . you. You are what's left when the thoughts stop . . . . the awareness away from thoughts is who you are . . . not trying to achieve anything . . . . just accepting what's there . . . . allowing it to be as it is.

That is all there is to say about how to stop thinking. And there is nothing else to think about.

AFFIRMATIONS

Today I will cease the mind racing which drains me of self-love. It has served me well as a tool to shield against my feelings but I no longer need this tool.

I am ready to accept all of me in this present moment because this is the way I can heal and come into the light and love of this present moment.

Bodywork

*How depression affects the body
and how to heal it*

Anyone who's experienced the blight of depression also understands the toll it takes on the body. In the midst of a full-blown depressive period, the very last thing we worry about is our physical well-being. I remember that some days just waking up and finding I was still alive seemed a miracle. Forget trying to remember to shop for fruit and vegetables as well, that's just not going to happen! But what if you discovered that taking care of your body was going to *help* you beat depression faster? Would that have any impact on how you take care of yourself?

Interestingly health isn't just affected by the way we tend to abuse our bodies when we're depressed, with behaviour such as excessive drinking, eating disorders, over-exercising, drugs, junk food and inactivity being common. Depression affects us physically for other reasons as well. They are:

1. Stored physical memories
2. The mind–body connection
3. Chronic stress

Let's explore these in turn and look at ways we can re-address the imbalance in the body without having to run a marathon or turn into a macrobiotic fanatic.

I will also introduce you to two other techniques to help repair the physical body:

1. Breath work
2. Anchoring the body

Three ways depression affects the body
1: Stored physical memories

Many sufferers from depression also suffer from physical symptoms. This has a medical name: somatoform. It's the result of the body storing pain. You may have suffered from somatoform without realizing it. Perhaps you have gone to the doctor to have some tests and then felt puzzled when the tests come back negative because you know you don't feel well. The symptoms can't be traced to a specific physical cause yet the pain you feel is very real. This pain can manifest as aches, chronic illness or physical tension.

As we saw in *Step 4, Discovering Your Inner Child*, the body stores memories and these memories signal themselves with automatic responses *even if we don't consciously link them with a specific memory.* Have you ever smelt a perfume and immediately been transported back in time? Or how about a certain song that suddenly reminds you of where you were years ago? It happens in a split-second. We might experience a feeling of déjà vu even though we can't consciously recall the memory. It has been explained as an event experienced as a sensory input and then stored into memory even though the conscious part of the brain has wiped out all details. When the same sensory trigger is released, the mind transports us back instantly, regardless of whether the memory is positive or negative.

The negative stored memory is activated when something happens to trigger the familiar but forgotten original sensory input. We might flinch when someone raises their arm to scratch their head or we get a lurch in our stomach if someone raises their voice. On a longer-term footing, if we're living under certain conditions which unknowingly remind us of old negative memories, we may be suffering from chronic physical discomfort.

For example, let's look at the story of Sally. When she was eight Sally's father lost his job and she had to move house and leave her school. She then lost her network of friends. A few months later the ongoing rows between her parents led to them splitting up. Sally knew that the loss of income contributed to this entire chain of events but, as it happened so long ago, she had forgotten all about it. However, lately Sally's been struggling to make ends meet, and her current experiences are triggering stored memories and the associated stresses without her having any real idea what's happening. For Sally, and for all of us, the body continues to react to something that happened long ago, because something still lives inside us, right in the nerve cells.

When things go wrong and we suffer from depression, old memories come to the surface. When we ruminate on how bad things are now, without knowing it we invite the memories to wake up. Our hopelessness can tell us that there's no point in trying to get better because that's the way depression works. We're in a familiar place, even though we don't know why. We can feel completely powerless. We become quite ashamed of these old feelings because we don't understand them. We don't know where they've come from and it makes us frightened. The pain feels like an alien, jumping out when it's not wanted. We may think we are going mad and end up isolating ourselves.

These stored memories are often the source of aches and pains, stiff necks, bumps and lumps, stomach aches, insomnia, incredible fatigue, night sweats, panic attacks, anxiety attacks and chronic depression. We may also become very obsessive or display compulsive behaviours. If you've suffered from chronic depression you may have suffered from similar traits.

Let's look at two ways to relieve these deep and painful memories: stored memory activity and a tool called EFT.

Stored memory activity

This activity is designed to link stored memories and a current incident that may have upset you. It's designed to release old memories which will help you to feel lighter and beat depression faster.

Open your journal and roughly draw out the following headings:

Current incident	The sensation/ feeling it created in me	The memory it's linked to from the past	What I learned at the time	The reality of what happened

Here are two examples of stored memories and their effects:

Current incident	The sensation/ feeling it created in me	The memory it's linked to from the past	What I learned at the time	The reality of what happened
I saw a child being slapped in a shop.	Tension and anger, feeling futile.	My parents slapping me and I couldn't do anything.	I thought I was useless and I felt victimized.	I say they were inappropriate in the way they disciplined me.
A work colleague told me a piece of work was not up to scratch for a presentation.	Sinking feeling in my stomach, felt sick, head hanging down.	Unable to understand any of my school work.	I was thick.	I wasn't motivated to work and I got into trouble for it but I moved schools every two terms so I could never keep up and that wasn't my fault.

Complete this activity whenever an incident has happened that has thrown you. You will gradually build a picture of your memory store so you will be able to bring in a reality check every time you find yourself upset about something that happened and don't know why. The more you do this the quicker you will bring yourself up to speed and old memories will no longer drive your reactions to things that happen today.

If you have the resources you may want to try other approaches to heal old memories. There's a whole school of thought that says that other kinds of Bodywork therapies can greatly help people who suffer from depression, stored memories and associated aches and pains. Massage, acupuncture, shiatsu, craniosacral therapy, Alexander Technique, reflexology and reiki are among many therapies that can help release old pain through physical touch.

There is one therapy that can be done straight way which seems to be growing in popularity to help people through emotional turmoil. It's called the Emotional Freedom Technique (EFT). This technique is a form of psychological acupressure which is based on the same energy channels used in traditional acupuncture. Acupuncture has been used with incredible success for over 5,000 years. It's still used extensively to treat sick people in Chinese hospitals and is gathering pace here in the West as an alternative medical treatment for various ailments, including back problems.

EFT works by a simple tapping with the fingertips to input kinetic energy to specific meridians on the head and chest while thinking about a specific problem. It uses positive affirmations at the same time. The combination of tapping the meridians and the positive affirmations works to clear the stored memories and emotional blocks from your body's energy system. It is said to restore the mind/body balance completely if done properly. There's no definitive research to prove this but it's certainly gaining credibility in helping people with emotional distress. There are many demonstrations on how to perform this technique on YouTube and it's simply a matter of watching one or two videos to understand how to do it properly.

2: Mind–body–emotion connection

The mind–body–emotion connection is a three-way relationship. Emotion is the result of the mind and body connecting. Here is a simple way to demonstrate the connection:

Imagine now, if you will, that the one thing you want in your life has just happened. You've won the lottery, your friend with whom you've had a horrid argument turns up unexpectedly with an apology and a beer, or you've been given the all-clear on a worrying health problem. Can you feel the change in your body? A little lighter? Or happier? However, it works the other way too. Imagine a less pleasant scenario like something happens to your pet or you lose your home; the response in the body is not pleasant. It may be a lurch in the stomach or even heart palpitations. (OK, stop thinking like that right now!)

If you suffer from chronic depression, there is a tendency to think negatively and this creates a lot of unhelpful emotions which make us more depressed.

The only thing we ever deal with is a thought

The thing that kicks off this whole cycle is a thought. A thought is the *only* thing we are ever dealing with. Depression is the result of a large accumulation of negative thoughts and no matter what problems we have, our experiences are only the outer effects of our inner thoughts. All of our experiences in our lifetime up into this point have been created by our thoughts. For example, self-criticism is thought on thought where we beat ourselves up for things like not reaching our goals, being who we think others will like or generally tell ourselves we're not good enough. We can drive ourselves into the ground through punishing thoughts which castigate us until we are, literally, emotionally disabled and unable to function like other people. We may think it's other people who've done this to us but it isn't, we have – unknowingly – brought it upon ourselves. When we fill our heads with self-criticism, we often attract other people into our lives who will confirm those thoughts by criticizing us too and confirming what we already knew. We can become so brain-washed by our thoughts that if someone gives us a compliment, we don't hear it; in fact we twist the words and hear it as another criticism. Thoughts produce feelings and we believe the feelings. However, if we don't have the thought we won't have the feeling. The feeling is an automatic response to the thought but, more importantly, the whole process is a chronic resistance to acceptance.

We may be frustrated or resentful because we have to do something we don't want to do. All the energy of the unspoken resentment towards someone else is so polluted that it harms us more than it harms anyone else. Then all we think about is how annoyed we are, and more emotions are stirred up to create inner

141

conflict. This reaction is an unwillingness to accept things as they are, which creates negative emotions. At this point it doesn't really matter whether we are right or wrong, whether or not the feelings are justified, or whether these thoughts are correct. The fact is we're resisting this very moment and thereby creating constant conflict. This conflict is like a pollutant, poisoning us and those around us. There's nothing that feeds depression faster than a stream of pollutants!

Come into the present moment

If we come into this present moment, in this split-second and this split-second and this split-second, we instantly stop the mind affecting our emotions. The mind is trying to spin off into the past or the future but we can stop 'thinking' and bring our awareness into now. We can gently ask ourselves: what's going on inside me at this moment? We can bring our attention into our body and scan our body for sensation, tension or emotion.

The mind will go crazy trying to compete with the attention we have given to the body. But our attention on the body is pulling us away from the frenetic mind. This action takes the power away from the mind and it reacts like a trapped animal. It tries to think us out of our present awareness. We can step away from our mind and look at it as if it were a spinning roundabout. We no longer have to see the world through our mind but through our body awareness. This is where the seat of our inner power lives. If we practise being in this moment, if only for a spilt second, that split-second will grow to a whole second, three seconds and by the time we get to a minute, we have reached nirvana!

Body Meditation

The following meditation is a simple way of reconnecting yourself with your body.

> Settle down in a comfortable, safe place lying on your bed or somewhere you won't be disturbed .... wrap up in a rug or something to make you cosy .... when you are comfortable close your eyes .... now bring

your attention to your breath . . . . and feel the rise
and fall of the abdomen as your breath moves in
and out . . . . Lie here for a moment and let your
breath be your guide . . . . As you breathe in and
out . . . . you may notice your mind is wandering
off in thoughts . . . . or that you experience physical
sensations in your body . . . . simply escort your mind
back to the breath and feel the breath going in . . . . and
out . . . . and in . . . . and out . . . . This is a meditation
to be fully aware of your body . . . . your experience.
It's not about trying to change anything . . . . or trying
to relax . . . . but the intention of this meditation is to
bring your awareness to the sensations in your body as
you touch each part of it with your attention . . . . Bring
your attention back to the rising and falling of your
abdomen . . . . and get a sense of the sensation of the
rise and the sensation of the fall as your breath moves
in and out of your body . . . . Bring your attention now
to your feet and ankles and wrap them up in a ball
of light . . . . and feel the connectedness between the
ankles and the balls of the feet . . . . and now focus your
attention on your toes . . . . and imagine your attention
as a magic wand . . . . and go in and out of all ten toes
feeling the sensation of each toe as you touch it with
your attention . . . . and now draw your attention to the
balls of the feet . . . . and bring your attention down
to the heels . . . . and now wrap your attention around
your ankles . . . . feel the lightness around the whole
of your foot and ankle . . . . and let your attention
linger on the sensation that surrounds your feet and
ankles . . . . When you are ready bring your attention to
your calves and your shins and allow your awareness
to expand through the whole of the lower part of your
leg . . . . swirling around the top of the ankles . . . . and
up to the top part of your lower leg . . . . let your
awareness stay with your whole lower leg . . . . Notice
the sensation you feel . . . . and accept the sensation

because there's no need to change anything.... Continue up your body when you're ready.... move on to your knees.... and your pelvic area.... and your hips.... and your lower back and abdomen and your upper back and chest.... then your neck and shoulders.... and now your upper arms.... your lower arms.... your hands and your head.... your mouth.... your nose.... and cheeks.... and eyes and crown of the head, becoming aware of all sensations and anything you may be resisting.... just bring your awareness into that more than anywhere else.... You can dissolve any tension using the breath.... by flushing the whole body with your full awareness starting from the crown of the head.... with the in breath take your attention all the way down to your feet and with your out breath bring your attention from your feet all the way back up to the top of your head.... Rest here until you are ready to open your eyes.

3: Dealing with chronic stress

There is a specific link between depression and stress. Not all of us suffer from acute stress when we are depressed but as a rule we all suffer from more stress than is good for us. We are becoming tolerant of higher stress levels: if someone walked into a doctor's surgery with modern-day 'normal' stress levels, 50 years ago they would have been diagnosed with a major stress disorder! Even if we're not a 'stressy' type, our higher stress levels could simply be down to modern life. With the pace accelerating all the time, it's hard not to be affected by our 24/7 lifestyle. By decreasing our stress levels, even if we think we don't feel stressed, we're going to beat depression faster.

What exactly is stress? It's a reflex which causes the heart to pound, creates butterflies in the stomach or coldness in the chest. This is an automatic response to a perceived threat. The threat doesn't even have to be real. As long as we think there is a threat, our body will react even if the threat is imagined. This instinctive stress response is known as 'fight or flight', a hard-wired reaction to perceived threats to our survival. When survival meant facing immediate and real threats such as confronting a charging lion, this response saved our lives. When our body senses danger its innate intelligence automatically takes charge by triggering a set of changes that bypass our rational thoughts. Priority is given to all physical functions which provide more power to face an enemy or to flee. The hormone adrenaline released at this time is fast-acting and powerful and activates this 'fight– flight' mechanism in the body, causing blood to flow away from the main organs to the limbs, stopping digestion and causing the heart to beat faster. It belongs to a group of hormones called catecholamines that help to keep the body on a high state of alert.

Charging lions are no longer a concern, unless you happen to be living in the wild! But the fight or flight response still works, though it is now triggered by different, seemingly less life-threatening events. Many day-to-day situations can set it off: moving home, a difficult boss, divorce, separation, demanding children, traffic jams, the fear of terrorism and others. The more often we are exposed to these types of stresses, the more over-active our fight or flight response becomes until we find ourselves operating at fever-pitch level, constantly prepared for battle, perceiving potential threats everywhere. That is why people who are over-stressed not only show physiological symptoms such as high blood pressure, rapid heart rate or shallow fast breath; they can seem overly sensitive or aggressive. Today many of us don't take enough physical exercise to 'burn off' the effects of our response and we're left with stress build-up. We learn to control our reactions, but this does not counteract the stress response.

How stressed are you?

Before we go any further, let's see if you are vulnerable to stress with this checklist from the Stress Management Society. Grab your journal and mark yourself from 1 (always applies to you) to 5 (never applies to you) to each statement:

1. I eat at least one hot, balanced meal a day.
2. I get seven to eight hours of sleep at least four nights a week.

3. I have at least one person who lives nearby from whom I can ask a favour.
4. I exercise to the point of perspiration at least twice a week.
5. I do not smoke.
6. I drink fewer than five alcoholic drinks a week.
7. I am the appropriate weight for my height.
8. I drink no more than two cups of coffee, tea or cola a day.
9. I have a network of friends, family and acquaintances on whom I can rely.
10. I confide in at least one person in my network about personal matters.
11. I am generally in good health.
12. I am able to speak openly about my feelings when angry, stressed or worried.
13. I do something for fun at least once a week.
14. I recognize stress symptoms.
15. I take quiet time for myself during the day.

Now add up your scores and take away 15. Under 5 – you are chilled. Skip this step! If you are between 5 and 20 then you have life in fairly good control but you do still have a vulnerability to stress and your body's 'shock absorbers' will need to deal with stress in a healthy non-aggressive way. If your score is between 20 and 50, then you are approaching the danger zone and you are vulnerable to stress . . . your relationships may be strained and you may not be operating in your most resourceful state. If your score is over 50, your stress level is very high and your health and well-being are in danger. You have potentially a lot of stress in your life but few ways to deal with it.

What is the link between stress and depression?

Well, they are entirely different but work together to make us feel . . . well . . . not so good and this starts off with feeling a lack of control. Do know that feeling when you're trying to hang on to people or things or situations and they keep slipping away from you? This is incredibly common when we feel depressed and it makes us unable to see a way of making things better. As our hopelessness increases, our stress levels increase too and once our stress goes up, we start to sleep badly and wake up feeling exhausted. This makes us more depressed, which leads to negative thinking and beating ourselves up. In turn we develop unhealthy habits like eating junk food or drinking or smoking a lot, which makes us more depressed and feeling more out of control – which starts the whole cycle over again.

But I'm sure you also know how you feel when you wake up rested and refreshed after a good night's sleep. That's where we want to get to and that's why it's important to tackle stress levels before anything else.

The stress and depression cycle

Let's look at one technique that can help decrease your stress levels. It's called **H.A.L.T.** This stands for **hungry, angry, lonely and tired** and there is no getting away from the fact that if you are feeling all these things at once then you are going to be stressed.

Hungry: of course, describes the most obvious physical condition of lack of food. We all know how important it is to have regular nutritious meals but did you know that the wrong foods can actually increase your stress levels? Start by limiting caffeine because that's one 'quick fix' that can make you burn and crash.

Angry: we also mean frustration, irritation, bottled-up feelings, resentment, fury and so on. Feeling angry and not being able to do anything about it leads to huge stress and depression so a quick approach to this is to see anger as an expression of an unmet need. What this means is that something you feel angry about could so easily be resolved by some action.

If you find yourself frustrated and stressed at work . . . what do you need to make that better? Perhaps you're frustrated with the kids . . . what do you need to make your life more manageable? Most of us have never learned how to express anger constructively so this can be quite a challenge . . . but you may feel liberated if you take your needs seriously.

Lonely: loneliness is very common in people who are stressed and depressed because we find it hard to reach out. But that old phrase, a problem shared is a problem halved, has never been truer because when you share your thoughts and feelings, you can unload and lighten up.

So, instead of having that extra glass of wine or switching on the TV for the evening, why not pick up the phone and talk to an old friend or join a group, 12-step meeting or club that will get you connecting with others and having some fun as well as reducing your loneliness.

Tired: there are many forms of tiredness that come from depression and stress. However, the one thing that guarantees an energy boost is exercise. Exercise really is an effective mood boost and it doesn't have to mean dragging yourself to the gym. You could ride a bike, dig the garden, go for a walk or a swim. Exercise boosts our endorphin levels, the 'happy hormones' that give up that good feeling when we've got up and got moving.

Often, when I'm stressed I'll automatically think HALT and I quickly realize that the conditions I've put myself in aren't conducive to my happiness and I need to take better care of myself. It's like an instant de-stressor.

A de-stress meditation

Here's a meditation designed to relieve stress. It's best if you listen with your own voice. Record into your phone, PC or tablet and remember that the dots represent pauses.

Get ready now by closing your eyes.... I want you to take a deep breath, so gently inhale and sigh it out.... And again.... Gently inhale and sigh it out.... Now locate a place in your body where you feel your breath most strongly – this may be your shoulder, rib cage or diaphragm or another place.... Now bring your attention to it.... and from this place begin to observe your breath.... and let it do whatever it wants to do.... allowing your breath to do whatever it wants to do.... When thoughts come up.... don't worry just realize they have and turn your awareness to your breath.... relaxing and allowing it to do whatever it wants to do.... Identify where there is a stress spot in your body.... It could be your back or your legs or your ribs.... wherever that is.... Now just like you did with your breath.... bring your attention to your stress spot and then.... do nothing.... just keep your attention on it and just allow the stress spot to do what it wants to do.... if thoughts come up don't worry it's fine. Just bring yourself back to your stress spot.... that's all you have to do.... Just relax into your stress spot and if you find your attention wandering again, don't worry.... just bring yourself back to your stress spot and relax.... allowing your stress spot to do whatever it wants to do.... Relax, allow and return.... watch how your stress spot dissolves.... the more you can allow it to dissolve by relaxing, the more it will dissolve.... relax, allow and dissolve.... allow your stress to dissolve itself.... The more you can relax and allow.... the more your stress spot will dissolve itself.... continue as often as you need to relieve your stress.... allowing, relaxing and

149

returning. . . . Now, open your eyes and smile because
your stress levels will be lower and you can return to
this meditation any time you feel stressed and want
an instant chill.

Repairing bodywork
1: Breath work

Breath work is an ancient ritual that helps to bring together
the mind and the body. The mysterious powers associated with
the breath are mostly unheard of in the West but Indian yogis
developed a science around certain breathing techniques that,
applied methodically over a period of time, would give specific
results. It's called pranayama and it's believed to be the vital
force that creates various currents of energy in the body that
affect moods and levels of stress and can resolve deep emotional
traumas. Recently, breath work has been used as a therapeutic
tool to affect positively not only the physical aspects of our bodies
but also the emotional and spiritual aspects as well.

Think about the way we droop during a depressive episode:
hunched shoulders, slumped posture, eyes down and head in
the hands. Our lungs collapse, making our breathing short and
shallow. This stops oxygen-rich blood sending oxygen around
the body. However, the good news is that learning to breathe
again enables your lungs to expand. This makes more oxygen
go into all parts of the body, which will make you feel better
instantly. (Did you just take a deep breath when you read that?
I did!)

There's no doubt that our emotions are linked to our breath.
When we're angry we pant and when we're happy we have a
more relaxed, open breath. People who suffer anxiety or panic
attacks talk about not being able to breathe or having to gulp
great lungfuls of air. If our breath changes with our emotions
then we can change our emotions with our breath. Although
regular breathing is an automatic function we can learn to
breathe deeper. This can help pull more oxygen into the whole
body making us feel lighter and calmer, which can help us feel
more centred.

This next activity helps to balance the breath. It's easy to do, can be done anywhere, any time, gives fast results and you could see a difference in literally two minutes. You can do it when you're travelling, at work, before going to bed or anywhere you have a few minutes to yourself.

> Sit in a comfortable position and place your hands on your knees. Drop your shoulders and then close your eyes. On your next breath out visualize the breath going out to the count of five. Pull in your stomach muscles to help your lungs to deflate. At the end of the breath count for two seconds then breathe in slowly by expanding your stomach muscles to the count of five. Repeat this between five and ten times.

2: Anchoring the body

This technique involves bringing the attention into the body to create instant 'peace of mind'.

When we are depressed we can often cut ourselves off from our body because our awareness is centred in thinking and this sets us spinning like a washing machine. We can forget we have a chest, heart and abdomen, legs and arms, hands and feet! We identify with the racing thoughts so much that we only give our body a cursory level of attention. Living in our thoughts creates an inordinate amount of stress because it constantly taps into our 'fight or flight' response and leaves us depleted of energy, wired and tired. By anchoring our awareness in our body we can instantly turn that habit round 180 degrees.

The idea of anchoring in the body is simply to take the focus of our attention away from our mind and direct it into our body. Once our attention is directed into the body it becomes the beginning of an inward journey that will take us to the source of our peaceful inner chamber. It can also help our life to feel more vibrant and powerful. It's an extraordinary experience that can change your whole way of being because your awareness no longer centres on your brain but on the heart – your spirit.

Here is a mindfulness activity which can help you reconnect

with your body. Record these words and play them back; your own voice is the most effective way to communicate with yourself. Remember that the dots represent a pause.

Close your eyes and concentrate on your breathing for a few seconds . . . . take a few moments to connect with your abdomen . . . . become aware of your abdomen going up and down as your breath flows in and out . . . . Bring your attention into your body and feel it from the inside out . . . . don't think, simply feel the body . . . . If you start to think simply escort your attention from your mind . . . . back down through your face . . . . through your neck . . . . through your chest and into your abdomen – the core . . . . Now as you focus your attention on the core . . . . a strong feeling will begin to vibrate . . . . right where your attention is focused . . . . See this sensation in the middle of you as a white ball . . . . which is growing . . . . the more attention you give it . . . . see this light spreading out from the centre of your core . . . . it's filtering down into your lower abdomen, down your thighs . . . . into your lower legs . . . . and into your feet . . . . all the way to the end of your toes . . . . See the light moving up into your chest cavity . . . . now into your neck . . . . up into the back of your head . . . . all the way to the top and down into your face and ears . . . . sense the light moving through your shoulders . . . . and down your arms to your elbows . . . . and into your lower arms . . . . and through your hands to your fingers . . . . now come back to the light . . . . in your abdomen . . . . Stay with the focus on this light . . . . and you will begin to see the energy emanating from the middle of you and spreading out and down through your legs . . . . up into your chest and head . . . . and all the way down your arms . . . . You may feel a slight tingling . . . . this is the vibration of the energy . . . . it's connected to the source of the universal energy . . . . Stay with this energy for a few more moments.... Now think about your dominant hand.... press the index finger and thumb together.... in your mind connect the energy from your finger and thumb towards the energy in the centre of you.... see a strong white line join the two.... wherever your hand moves the line follows.... visualize the line getting stronger.... see the source of the light in your centre sending energy to your fingers like a powerful pulse.... Relax your hands now and gently open your eyes.

You now have an anchor from your power source to your conscious world. Whenever you remember, reconnect yourself to this power source with your finger and thumb. It will bring you back to your centre and away from your mind. When you stop for a few minutes, instead of thinking about something you have to do later, simply escort your attention back into the body and anchor it. After you sit down and before you switch on the TV, or when you get in the car and shut the door, or after you've jumped on the bus ... just pause and bring your attention back into your body. This becomes a self-fulfilling prophecy because the more you do it the more fantastic it feels.

There is a direct and fast correlation between bringing your attention into the body and the release of the feel-good hormones. Once you begin to do this activity on a regular basis the next step is always to have 10% of your attention focused on your body; even when you are having a conversation with another person, learn to keep 10% of your attention in your body. You will build deep roots inside you, building self-confidence, happiness and a better perspective on life.

AFFIRMATIONS

I trust in the process of life which leaves me free to become friends with my body.

I lovingly take care of my body, it is my friend and it is the divine expression of me.

I create new patterns which serve to bring me peace, harmony and vitality.

Dynamic Foods

To lift depression in 72 hours

C an the answer to depression really lie in food? Yes it can. People may have told you to get out and have fun, socialize and have a good time getting drunk, but that could make you feel worse. What they didn't tell you was that feeling good could lie in some pretty special foods that don't mean spending your way out of depression. These are dynamic 'depression fighting' foods that have specific properties to stimulate certain hormones and fan the flames of happiness.

We've often seen the female lead in a romantic comedy drown her sorrows in a tub of ice cream and there are the long running jokes about chocolate improving women's PMS symptoms and general mood. But there's a downside and here's what happens:

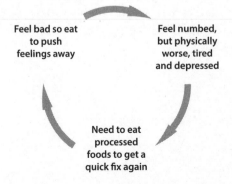

Feel bad so eat
to push
feelings away

Feel numbed,
but physically
worse, tired
and depressed

Need to eat
processed
foods to get a
quick fix again

When we feel depressed it's easy to tuck into a bag of sweets or a plate of chocolate biscuits because they raise our blood sugar levels and seem to give us a 'lift'. After a short time, however, our blood sugar levels will suddenly drop, leaving us feeling grumpy, fatigued and craving more sugar. This is because the pancreas secretes high amounts of insulin to prevent a dangerous spike in blood sugar levels. The only way out seems to be to have another couple of biscuits or a lie down!

The current understanding about the happiness/depression food connection starts with the 'emotional chemicals' and how they affect the brain. The very act of eating food produces brain chemicals that make us feel warm and satisfied. These chemicals are called neurotransmitters. Their function is to send messages from one nerve cell to another within the brain and they influence thought, functions and feelings. These chemicals are made in the brain from the food we eat and are highly sensitive to food. In fact, they get all their nutrients from the food we eat so if we don't eat the right foods, our brain can't help but under-perform.

This chapter will help you identify if your diet is contributing to your depression. It then looks at which foods can help beat depression and which foods you should try to give up if you want to beat depression *faster*.

Is your diet making you depressed?

If you're not sure whether your food is affecting your emotions, here's a simple questionnaire which will get you thinking about how much your diet may be contributing to how you feel. Score yourself in the boxes on the right and review the results as explained below.

Question	Every day: 3 points	2/3 times a week: 2 points	Rarely: 1 point
Do you eat more than one high sugar snack e.g. piece of cake or a couple of biscuits?			
Do you have more than one small alcoholic drink?			
Do you eat less than two portions of fresh fruit or vegetables a day?			
Do you feel tired after you have eaten a meal?			
Do you drink less than two glasses of water?			
Do you rely on convenience foods for your main meals?			
Do you eat in front of the television?			
Do you suffer from headaches after eating?			
Do you grab some snack food when you are hungry?			
How often do you go without a piece of fresh fruit?			
How often do you eat fried foods?			
Do you feel bloated after eating a meal?			
Do you ever feel depressed about the food you eat?			
Do you keep breaking promises to yourself about eating better?			
Do you ever miss breakfast?			
How often do you go through the day on snacks rather than 3 meals a day?			
Do you feel depressed after eating?			
How often do you skip main meals?			
Do you eat high salt foods, e.g. a bag of crisps/nuts?			
How often do you eat takeaway meals?			
TOTAL			

Scoring

1–20   Your eating habits are generally healthy; it is
       unlikely that your diet is depressing your mood.
       You are not allowing too much processed food into
       your diet.

21–40 Your diet is probably contributing to your
       depression. You may have erratic eating habits which
       could exacerbate stress and when you get stressed
       you may find yourself relying on quick-energy
       foods that may not be contributing to your overall
       well-being and leave you feeling hungry more often.

41–60 Your diet is unbalanced which means that you are
       probably eating high amounts of salt/sugar/saturated
       fats, all of which definitely contribute to depression.
       If you feel depressed you may find yourself turning
       to processed foods for comfort and these kind of
       foods can create a 'numbing out' effect and cause
       you to lose mental focus and clarity. Once you find
       yourself in this vicious cycle, your craving for highly
       processed foods becomes strong and it can become
       hard to break the habit. There is a high probability
       that changing your food will change your mood.

Which dynamic foods beat depression?

One recommendation for nourishing our bodies to boost our mood is to implement the 'five a day' rule. Scientific studies from the World Health Organization recommend eating a minimum of five portions of fruit and vegetables a day. Fruits and vegetables help to protect us from illnesses that take time to develop. What we eat now will affect our health in twenty years' time – the time taken for some illnesses, such as heart disease and cancer, to develop. A portion is as much as we can hold in our hand.

It's a double-edged sword: our immune system is weakened by chronic stress, which is a symptom of depression – but continued suppression of the immune system can lead to illness. People who are ill are more likely to feel lethargic and debilitated, and lethargy and debilitation can lead to depression.

By way of contrast, happy people make for healthy people. One study has shown that feeling good reduces the risk of disease. 'There's a direct link between how we're feeling and the biological processes which relate to illness and illness risk,' said Dr Andrew Steptoe, the British Heart Foundation Professor of Psychology at University College, London. 'Biology is going to be on the side of those people who are going to be in a more positive state of mind, and it may well stand these people in good stead for their future health.'

By making sure we keep ourselves healthier, we are helping ourselves stay happier. In fact, the evidence shows that eating at least five portions of fruit and vegetables each day has very real health benefits – it could help prevent up to 20% of deaths from our nation's biggest killers – heart disease and some cancers.

Six key nutrients to help beat depression

Let's look at a list of six key nutrients for helping to fight depression and where to find them.

Tryptophan

Foods rich in the amino acid tryptophan facilitate the body's uptake of the wonderful neurotransmitter serotonin. We want plenty of serotonin to feel good and beat depression. High tryptophan foods are:

- Soy products: soy milk, tofu, soybean nuts
- Seafood
- Turkey
- Whole grains
- Beans
- Rice
- Houmous
- Lentils
- Hazelnuts, peanuts
- Eggs
- Sesame seeds, sunflower seeds

Omega-3

Omega-3 fatty acids are another type of compound which has been proven to lift depression. This important nutrient is critical for good health. Omega-3 compounds are a form of polyunsaturated fats, one of four basic types of fat that the body derives from food. All polyunsaturated fats, including the omega-3s, are increasingly recognized as important to human health but they cannot be produced by the body, which means they need to be provided by our diet. A lack of Omega-3 mood-boosting nutrients may lead to depression and other mental health problems.

Here is a list of the gorgeous Omega-3 fat sources:

- Fish
- Canola oil
- Olive oil
- Flaxseed oil
- Walnuts
- Venison

Folic acid

Folic acid is also a brilliant depression fighter and research shows that people with low levels of folic acid are more like to suffer from depression. Scientists at the UK Medical Research Council recommend plenty of folic acid daily as a preventative measure for depression. Folic acid is a water-soluble vitamin and the body can't retain it for long, with any excess being expelled in the urine. This means that any of us could be deficient in folic acid at any one time; it is a hard vitamin to keep in the body. Eating some of these foods will help keep your levels high.

- Beetroot
- Spinach
- Broccoli
- Avocados
- Asparagus
- Dried beans
- Brussels sprouts

Magnesium

Magnesium deficiency has been strongly linked to depressive symptoms. It is necessary for the absorption of calcium and is the primary mineral required by the adrenal glands to help the body cope with stress. Increasing your magnesium levels could help with muscle cramps, sleep problems, fatigue and depression. Eat some of these foods to add magnesium to your diet:

- Spinach
- Avocados
- Barley
- Pumpkin seeds
- Sunflower seeds
- Brazil nuts
- Buckwheat, almonds

Vitamin B6

Vitamin B6 is a particularly brilliant vitamin for helping reduce susceptibility to mood changes and is a good mood-enhancer, excellent for irritability, aids good sleep and helps alleviate depression. Foods high in B6 include:

- Sweet potatoes
- Wholegrains
- Tofu
- Nuts
- Seeds
- Pulses
- Avocados
- Apricots
- Asparagus

Vitamin D

This is called the sunlight vitamin because the body produces it when the sun's ultraviolet B (UVB) rays strike the skin. It is the only vitamin the body manufactures naturally and is technically considered a hormone. Vitamin D has been a key nutrient to help Seasonal Affective Disorder (SAD) sufferers and one study found that people with SAD who received increased amounts of Vitamin D achieved a significant improvement in depression symptoms – albeit after one month. Foods high in Vitamin D are:

- Prawns
- Milk
- Cod
- Eggs

Vitamin D supplements are cheap and easy to obtain and a wise investment for helping to beat depression.

Five main foods types to cut out (or at least cut down on)

It's not just what we eat; it's also what we cut out. When we look at the foods that cause depression, there is no doubt that a high fat, salt and sugar diet is going to affect our mood badly. Much research has shown that certain foods negatively affect our mood and our modern diet of processed foods contributes to the body feeling lethargic, stressed and depressed.

Sugar

If there's one main culprit it's sugar. The reason sugar has such a negative impact on depression is that it causes a rise in the insulin levels of the blood. This also raises the serotonin level in the brain. Sugar thus causes the body to have an artificial, chemical, mental high which results in an artificial lift in mood. But continuous large doses of sugar over a long time usually cause the brain's serotonin production to slow or shut down. When the body cuts back on serotonin production it reduces the amount of serotonin available at any given time. The lack of serotonin in the brain causes depression.

If an individual is a high sugar eater, to maintain a normal level of serotonin in the brain the individual must eat more and more sugar to avoid the feeling of depression and maintain a normal mood. This causes the swinging cycle of 'sugar high/ sugar low' and ensures that the body then needs more sugar to feel 'normal'. In many ways, this cycle is similar to alcohol dependency when the alcoholic needs more and more alcohol to achieve the same effect that the alcohol once had; conversely, the more alcohol that is consumed, the more the body tolerates it and so the need for higher consumption increases.

Continuously high levels of sugar create an artificial energy which we have become used to and may have always felt. It is hard to escape sugar as even powdered baby milk contains sugar and this will give us the taste for it from a very early age. However, the craving for sugar is beatable and within three days you may notice a profound difference in your mood and your craving as you turn to other foods.

Salt

Too much salt inhibits good kidney function and unhappy kidneys can lead to depression and fatigue. We need our kidneys to feel energetic and if our kidneys can't do their job we end up feeling enervated, we suffer lower back pain, experience feeble knees and we have to keep going to the toilet because our bladder is weak. Usually the salt is deposited in the joints, particularly the knees, which may result later in arthritis and rheumatism. It makes no difference where the salt has come from, whether table salt or in processed foods, the results are the same. If our kidneys are not functioning adequately, we do not feel good and not feeling good on a long-term basis can lead to a depressed mood.

On average we eat around 9–12 grams of salt a day. Government guidelines tell us not to have more than 6g of salt a day (a flat teaspoon). Three-quarters of the salt we eat comes from processed food, such as breakfast cereals, soups, sauces, ready meals, biscuits – and almost everyone eats some processed foods. Even people who make all their own meals from scratch will usually buy foods such as bread and biscuits that can be high in salt. Taking this into account, we should only add a further 1.5g of salt per day to our cooking, which is about the same weight as a paperclip. According to the British Nutrition Foundation (BNF), if we were to reduce salt intake to 6g a day, about 20% fewer people would get strokes and 15% fewer would get heart attacks. We are talking about 20,000–30,000 people saved every year. In fact the BNF has calculated that if we were to go on a diet consisting purely of natural meats, fruits and vegetables, with no salt added, our sodium intake would drop by 80–85%. Of course, we add salt to food, but this only accounts for a surprising 15–20% of the salt we consume in total. This huge intake of salt is contributing to our stress, lethargy and depression.

Bad fats

Many Western countries have a love affair with high fat foods: chips, deep-fried fish, fried chicken, deep-fried potato skins. We adore doughnuts, biscuits, cakes and pastries, especially when the smell wafts out from the bakery section. What makes them taste so good? They all contain saturated and trans fats. This is what gives them that delicious, rich, mouth-watering, mood altering, fatty taste. It's the good, the bad and the ugly all rolled into one: they taste delicious but we know they are bad for our health. Did you also know that they can really affect the way you feel and deplete you of energy, brightness and a bountiful mood?

A recent study by scientists from the University of Las Palmas de Gran Canaria and the University of Granada found that consumers of fast food are 51% more likely to develop depression than minimal or non-consumers. Moreover, the connection between the two is so strong that 'the more fast food you consume, the greater the risk of depression', said Almudena Sánchez-Villegas, lead author of the study.

The results also demonstrated that those who ate the most fast food were more likely to be single, less active and have poor dietary habits, and it was also common for individuals in this group to smoke and work over 45 hours per week.

So what's the answer? Here are some ideas: buy skim milk, your taste buds will adapt. Try baking, steaming, poaching or grilling instead of frying. Limit butter and use spray olive oil for cooking. Twice a week replace red meat with beans. For desserts use fat-free ice cream, frozen yogurt or sorbet.

Dairy

How do dairy foods impact on our mood? We have been brought up to assume that milk and its by-products are good for us. A warm glass of milk before bed is nurturing, a chunk of cheese with some bread is a regular snack, and a cream cake is a gorgeous treat. But what is the downside?

Dairy products are high in saturated fats which can increase blood cholesterol and cause poor circulation to the brain, inhibiting the synthesis of neurotransmitters. As these neurotransmitters, such as serotonin, play such a vital role in the way we feel, any malfunction in their performance will negatively impact on our mood.

Many of us are allergic to lactose which is found in all dairy foods. If we eat foods that we can't tolerate, and our bodies can't digest, the partially broken-down food molecules produced get up to terrible mischief in the body. Sometimes they create inflammation in the skin or joints or organs. And sometimes they disrupt those precious vital processes which allow us to cope and stay happy. So ditch the ice cream and discover dairy-free wonders in the freezer cabinet.

White flour

White bread is a bona fide promoter of depression. It's made from stripped white flour, which is a refined carbohydrate with a sky-high GI factor (glycaemic index). GI is a ranking of carbohydrate-containing foods based on their overall effect on blood glucose levels. Slowly absorbed foods have a low GI rating, whilst foods that are more quickly absorbed have a higher rating. This is important because choosing slowly absorbed carbohydrates, instead of quickly absorbed carbohydrates, can help even out blood glucose levels when you have depression and this will help to stabilize our mood.

White flour is so refined that it has been robbed of its original, natural elements such as fibre, healthy oils, vitamins and minerals. This refined carbohydrate is so depleted of most of its nutrients that bakeries are required by law to add them back in artificially.

Have you ever had a sandwich for lunch, made with white bread, and then felt as though you needed an afternoon nap because you were so tired?

That is probably a lot to do with the white bread that you ate. White bread has had most of its fibre removed. The gorgeous husk and wheat germ of the grain is no longer present and this makes a slice of white bread a very difficult food to navigate though the stomach. Lack of fibre in white bread can cause constipation, which is a horrible condition, leaving the sufferer feeling irritable, tired, sluggish and generally miserable. No wonder we feel drained and lethargic. In addition, white flour is so stripped of the natural selenium and oils that come from the ground that we don't receive the essential mood boosters that come from whole foods. It is also deficient in chromium (essential for blood-sugar control), zinc, iron and B vitamins which are immune boosters and depression busters.

Look for lower GI breads – the best varieties are the coarse grain kinds: stone-ground, whole-wheat, wholemeal, rye.

ACTIVITY: WRITING A FOOD JOURNAL

Why not try switching a few foods and see how much better you feel in three days. Start with recording your food and beverage intake so you can track how you feel based on what you've eaten.

Day	Place	Food/beverage	Time Place	Mood before	Mood after

Mood suggestions: depressed, overwhelmed, happy, anxious, peaceful, angry, sad, childlike, lonely, bored, thrilled, jealous, and hopeful.

- My day in review _____
- What triggered any cravings _____
- What I need to work on _____

Meditation: Mindful eating

This is a meditation to take us from mindless eating to mindful eating. The food we eat becomes who we are and this helps us to focus on our food and feel gratitude for this food. The benefits of mindful eating are that food tastes better when you pay attention; you enjoy it more; you eat less because you're not eating mindlessly; you experience a little oasis of calm; and you begin to address the emotions around eating.

Create the right space for the eating meditation and do just one thing – eat. Whatever you put in front of you consider it before you eat it. Notice the colour, texture, shape and smell. Take a moment to consider where it's come from and how it got to your table. Imagine it being planted, grown, picked and transported to you. If it's meat-based, what animals gave their life for you. Feel the blessings.

Take a bite and savour the texture and taste. Is it salty, sweet or acidic? Is it chewy, tough, soft or crunchy? Is it liquid or grainy? Can you taste the earth or the chemicals? Is it nourishing you as you swallow it? Consider all the nourishment it's giving your body. There's no judgement or criticism, just an acceptance of the food exactly as it is.

AFFIRMATIONS

I forgive myself for not treating my body as well as I could have; I did not know better at the time.

I listen to my body and give it what it needs even if I feel unhappy.

I will always keep some of my attention in my body; this will keep me rooted in the earth like a magnificent tree.

Cultivating Happiness

*Eight ways to keep depression-free
and stay happy*

C ontrary to popular opinion, happiness is not about winning the lottery or landing that perfect boyfriend/ girlfriend. No, it's more than that – much, much more. Happiness is a state of mind, according to the new Positive Psychology movement and we can cultivate it. The secret to happiness is recognizing that it lies in 'the now'. Or in other words, happiness lies inside each of us, not outside of us. And we can tap into that abundant happiness any time we like. The reason? Because 'the now' is free from worry and fear.

We live in an 'I want it now' world but what we really want is happiness. We want to win the lottery so we can put aside all our financial fears and we want that perfect relationship so we can feel loved. But these things are focusing our minds into the future and it's a leap we can never make because when we get into tomorrow, we are back in the now. So we wind ourselves up trying to imagine how we'll feel when we get there and all the while we could have that now.

The only hiccup in this theory for those of us who have suffered deep depression is that we have put a lot of obstacles in the way of our happiness, like constantly beating ourselves up or trying to control the depression. This is what other people don't realize – we would be happy if we could but we can't. We didn't mean to cement those obstacles in; it was if they just cemented themselves! No one had ever taken the time to explain how to dislodge them. And we needed someone else to tell us because if we'd known how to do it, we would have done. No one likes staying depressed because it's the worst place in the world.

However, now we're on *Step 10*, we have some insight into how we're allowing the depression to keep us in the fog. The key to happiness is removing the obstacles. Happiness is sitting waiting for us. It's been there since the day we were born. Some days we remember happy times and we want them back. The exciting thing is that it's not complicated. This step succinctly maps out eight things that we can do to cultivate happiness and stay depression-free.

As we recover from depression, our field of vision changes until we eventually see the reasons why we became depressed in the first place. Then we can follow a new path.

1: Not trying to beat depression

It's not our depression that keeps us stuck; it's the reaction to our depression that traps us. It's as if we identify with the depression and we are a depressed person – nothing more – just a depressive. And then we try to fix it, or wrench our way out of it, constantly fighting against it hoping that we can *pull ourselves together*. But if you have suffered chronic depression, you know that doesn't work.

We're not a 'depressed person', we simply have depressive symptoms. Accepting that is the key. Being depressed is a natural phenomenon for humans. We don't have to fight it, just accept that we are depressed without defining ourselves as only depressed and nothing else. We are so much more; we are joy, creativity and love. By allowing the depression to run its natural course, it will lift. Trying to force ourselves into a state of happiness isn't going to work. We don't have to try because happiness is waiting for us.

The only thing that feeds our depression is our mind

The one thing that feeds the depression is our mind-racing or rumination. Negative thinking produces past regrets and worry about the future. We try and figure it all out and struggle to fix the emotions by suppressing them. It doesn't take long before the depression has developed into a fully fledged monster.

So, the key is to disengage from the mind. Yes, you have permission to do that! You don't have to think at all. Just be. Mindfulness will take you there, to a place of peace and – yes happiness. Mindfulness is about being aware of the struggle but not *doing* anything about it. Your inner resources will help rebalance your state of being from a lopsided 'all in the head' person to a more stable position. And acceptance will allow you to be the person you are, whether you are depressed or not. These two approaches will help to create a space inside you to allow all that is meant to be.

2: Closing the door on the past

It's a human trait to assume that the past will determine the future and that we have little power over it. This suggestion can make us feel pretty powerless. Freud, the founding father of psychiatry, first developed this thesis and it has dominated much of our thinking ever since. But many researchers are now questioning whether an exhaustive examination of your past will actually help you live a happier present. In fact, hanging on to the past may be a signal that it's time to let it go.

Although childhood traumas can have a major impact on us, there are many people who've had similar traumas yet have found a way of not allowing them to ruin their adult lives. How have they done that? The new science of Positive Psychology states that events from childhood only affect our adulthood if we choose to believe the criticisms and misconceptions (given to us as children) and continue to nurture the associated negative emotions.

I know from my own perspective that when I dwell on the past and ruminate on my unhappy experiences, my negative feelings from the past begin to loom large again. The problem is trying to parcel them back up. I'd rather not have the experience at all and get on with focusing on my new, peaceful and contented self. If what we focus on grows, I'm happy to focus on moment to moment awareness and bliss.

As long as we're hanging on to the past, we're hanging on to emotional negativity. We all have a story and if we keep that alive by continuing to think we were hard done by, we also keep all the emotional reaction that manifests in the body alive. The body doesn't distinguish between a past and present threat, it simply reacts to all threats in the same way, even if they are only in the mind.

All past pain can be dissolved in the present moment

To close the door on the past all we have to do is recognize the pain or anger or depression we feel in our bodies *now* and mindfully stay with this moment until our attention dissolves it. All past pain can be dissolved in the present moment. Once we've held the space for the pain to just 'be' in our bodies, it will leave us because it's been acknowledged. It's like a baby who cries for attention: when it gets a cuddle, it stops crying. This is turning the old theories on their head but this is how to heal past pain – fast.

3: Not allowing expectations to rise

There's a distinct difference between happiness and pleasure. Happiness is the feeling we experience when we're balanced, blissful, peaceful and contented. It's what we were born with. We have the potential to reach it whenever our attention is in this moment. Pleasure is what we feel when we get something external like a new car, a book deal or a pay rise. Pleasure could be relabelled 'excitement' and it would make more sense. When we get what we want it might give us the illusion of 'happiness' because we get a natural high as the endorphins kick in. But once that high has evaporated, we go back into needing the next 'high' to lift us into that pleasure again. Worse still, if we don't get what we want, we might slip back into depression. This perpetuates the myth that it takes something outside us to 'make us happy'.

Many of us have lurched from one moment of pleasure to the next looking for the holy grail of pleasures finally to make the depression go away. But that hasn't happened. No matter how many fast cars, wardrobes of designer clothes or perfect careers we've tried to achieve, the bottom line is that we come home *to us*.

The true source of our happiness arises from our connections to our self in this present moment. When we focus on material 'highs' we raise our expectations, which leads to stress, anxiety, anger or fear. We set up a disconnection with this present moment and a focus on how we can get what we want in the future. Of course, this future is also a fantasy because when we get there, we're back here in *this moment*.

When we refocus on our own divinity, our loving parent and our inner child in this moment, we become calm and relaxed, the sure sign of happiness. By cultivating a mindfulness practice we increase our lasting happiness. If we rush through life we fail to experience the sweetness of life. We work on auto-pilot; it's called 'mind-less-ness'. But when we operate mindfully, we slow down our mind, which stops the jumping around, and we're free to smell the beautiful fragrance of a flower, watch the extraordinary work of a bee, or feel incredible love from another.

For me, when I stopped *trying to be happy,* and didn't let that expectation rise, I found myself lighter and more carefree. This is my freedom, the freedom to be who I am, not what I think I should be, and that includes 'happiness'. By lowering my expectations of myself, I find peace and serenity. Turns out, that's what I was looking for all along!

4: Building resilience

Resilience or the ability to 'bounce back' after encountering problems is an essential trait. Inevitably, life will throw up some apparently adverse situations, and being able to deal with such circumstances in a positive and creative way is often a measure of how happy and successful a person is.

Scientific studies have shown that resilient people show lower levels of depression. They are more likely to develop and grow as a result of adversity than people with low levels of resilience. Resilience is the ability to bounce back after encountering life problems and, self-trust is what grows, the more resilient you become. Being able to deal with adverse situations in a positive and creative way helps to cultivate security and increases happiness. Studies show that the more resilience we have the less likely we are to suffer from long-term depression. If we don't think we have a lot of resilience it can be learned. It could be argued that depression is a form of resilience, a way of protecting ourselves from feelings that we can't handle at the moment. So how do we turn that action round and make it work for us to beat depression?

It starts with self-trust and self-trust is about building our relationship with our self. Building and maintaining a good relationship with ourselves is no different to maintaining a successful relationship with a partner or friend. Maintaining relationships takes time, good communication and effort. When we become depressed we have lost the ability to communicate with ourselves, which can lead to the perception that we are abandoned. So how do we do it?

We need to talk to ourselves as if we are talking to another person. We should try to create a dialogue involving our higher power our loving parent and our inner child. Learning to connect and communicate with all three parts of you will guide you away from depression and towards a happy heart. The loving parent is the part of you that is gentle and soft but firm, and works with the higher power only for your good. The child is the heart of you where all your feelings live and this is the part of you that needs taking care of by the other two.

Begin to talk to yourself. Ask yourself questions in a loving way. Answers will come and, if you don't know how to respond, you simply ask your higher power for help. For example you might ask the child how he is feeling today and he might answer that he's feeling angry. You can then ask him why he is feeling angry and he will tell you. Because an expression of anger is usually about a need that hasn't been met, you can ask your higher power to show you how to get that need met. If your child is feeling depressed you can talk to the child, telling him that the depression is OK and won't be around for ever and ask your higher power to help to comfort the child.

This is a promise: the results will be astonishing and you will feel the difference immediately. If you don't believe this you may need a little blind faith until you get the hang of it. Once you start doing this your resilience will build and self-trust will grow. Practise this whenever you remember. I practise this all the time by having an internal dialogue with myself. It has become second nature and my confidence has developed like a small oak tree buried inside me that grows each day. Lovely!

5: Give up self-judging

Happiness comes from accepting our self and acceptance comes from giving up self-judging. Self-judging comes from our inner 'Jiminy Cricket' who sits on our shoulder like a critical, babbling, niggly voice telling us everything that's wrong about us. This has been learned but can also be un-learned. This voice is totally pointless and has no value or place in our life. It usually appears when we feel most vulnerable.

We all experience this voice, but those of us who've suffered crippling depression have it *screaming* in our ear. We may think it's useful and that if we didn't have it we might become lazy. But that's the critical voice talking. We won't become lazy, only happy, and we get a lot more productive when we're happy! The critical voice isn't useful and doesn't help us move forward; it only holds us back. It's not our real voice but one we've borrowed from someone else and it's time to hand it back. We don't need it and it's time for it to go.

The way to extricate this voice is to replace it with our loving parent. When we notice our self spiralling into a whirl of critical thoughts we can introduce the loving parent and stop the process instantly with an antidote! The critical voice is usually going over and over the same three or four critical thoughts: you'll never be happy; you can't do anything; no one cares about you. The loving parent comes with the voice of reason, compassion and understanding. If you think of counter-statements – you can be happy now; you can achieve tons of new things; many people care about you but I love you the most – you can work to replace the old message with a new one. And yes this is the 'work'. It's a doing-it-every-day, all-the-time, whenever-you-remember type of work because it doesn't happen on its own.

What if we can't monitor our thoughts? It is difficult to do this but here's the thing: our thoughts manifest into feelings so that's how we know what we're thinking. If we're feeling depressed then we're thinking negative thoughts. If we're feeling light and happy it's because we're thinking lovely thoughts. So when we feel depressed, we can track back to what our thoughts were and then we've caught them! From there we can challenge them and dismiss them. Then sit back and watch the good things arrive.

Post-it note it

One tip is to strike down critical thoughts with Post-it notes. Identify the most common Jiminy Cricket message. Write down the opposing message on a Post-it note. Put it somewhere you will see it, like next to your bed or on the bathroom mirror. Every time you walk by just take a moment to read it. They say it takes 21 days to replace an old thought with a new thought. Imagine that – 21 days and you're free of your self-critic. After 21 days, find the next most prominent message and repeat.

6: Saying yes to the depression, the suffering, the universe

When we suffer, our natural reaction is to stop the suffering by denying it. This doesn't work. We've been trying to stop the suffering for a long time. If it had worked we wouldn't be here. Instead of denying it, we embrace it. The secret is not to try and rationalize why we should stop the suffering because we're back into rumination. The key is to allow the suffering to be just as it is and to bring awareness into the present moment. The present moment will dissolve our suffering. This is old Buddhist wisdom, based on thousands of years of experience, that accepting the suffering dissolves it fast and opens the heart to healing.

When we say yes to the universe, we trust that, whatever our situation is, we can accept it. We learn to trust and build confidence in ourselves, which teaches us that whatever the universe brings to us we are willing to learn from it rather than saying no to it. When we say yes to the universe we are saying yes to life and it's so much easier to live this way than the alternative. It's a risk, but once we begin to take the risk of saying yes it becomes much easier and the obstacles are released and life begins to flow. There is much wisdom in the saying 'When one door closes, another door opens.'

7: The power of gratitude

Gratitude is powerful! It's so powerful that many studies have been commissioned to research how gratitude helps cultivate happiness. The results have determined that people who consciously acquire a positive gratitude outlook have improved health, good relationships and emotional balance. Feeling grateful for what we have energizes us, brings out our creativity and transforms our life. It helps us to give up feeling like a victim, buffeted by others and events. The word gratitude comes from the Latin word *gratia* which means grace, graciousness, or gratefulness. Gratitude is all of these rolled into one and it's a thankful appreciation for the goodness we've received. Gratitude can also help us to connect to something larger than us: people, nature, or a higher power.

Of course, if we've suffered from depression it's not easy to cultivate gratitude. Depression tends to make us think we're the ones who've had to put up with life's hardships and it's almost impossible to see what we've got to be grateful for. Becoming grateful can take a little time. Once we get over the resentment about 'having to be grateful' we can start to write one thing a day that we feel grateful for. Just being able to sit quietly and write the words in a book is a soulful place to be and we may feel grateful simply for that. Other ways to find gratitude are to write a letter to someone who's done something for us when we didn't have the opportunity to thank them, or write about a good time in which we remember feeling happy. Or we could just acknowledge the tiny little things that life brings us which we so easily overlook: when the sun comes out, bird song, someone making us a cup of coffee, the smell of a lilac bush, someone laughing at one of our jokes.

In Positive Psychology research, gratitude is strongly and consistently associated with greater happiness. It helps people cultivate happiness, experience more positive emotions, enjoy good experiences, improve health, develop resilience to deal with adversity, and build strong relationships. What's not to love!

8: Practise mindfulness all day long

It's easy to say 'I'll practise being mindful when I've got nothing else on.' This is especially true when looking at what we do at work. Many of us look at work as something we have to *get through* until we get home and then we can be happy. Or we're working as hard as we can so we can give it all up and then we can find peace. Just to give you a heads-up here, many of the retirees I've spoken with say that they were sorely disappointed. They say that when they got to retire, the promise (set by them) that they would finally be content, blissful and happy – never came true. They actually felt worse because not only did they not feel happier but now they didn't have work to distract them from just how depressed they were!

Here's another approach. Why not practise being mindful whenever you remember? Trying to separate mindful living from *work* or other tasks like looking after children, taking care of elderly relatives, or when the house is finished, is like waiting until you die before you can rest. By bringing mindfulness into the 'every day, every hour, every minute' you can transform your life. There is no need to sit in a cave and meditate for ten years because mindfulness can bring you to that same wavelength quickly. You will discover that your levels of tension and stress will decrease, and your levels of satisfaction will soar. Looking into the future to *save you* from the awfulness of what's going on now will diminish. Finding pleasure in just being 'you' will surprise you, and regrets you had about past issues will leave you.

Practising Mindfulness All Day Long With: S.L.O.W.

S Slow down thoughts until they come to a stop
L Lead your attention to your breath
O Observe this moment and be fully present
W When the mind wanders, bring it back and repeat

Walking meditation

A walking meditation is any meditation in action. We use the experience of walking as our focus and we become mindful of our experience whilst walking. It may help to be guided through this meditation and you can record the meditation into a phone or another device and listen to it while you walk.

When you step outside simply stand on the spot and become aware of your weight being evenly distributed to the soles of your feet and down into the earth. Become aware of how you adjust your body so you stand upright. These adjustments are constant – just become aware of them. And now you can begin to walk at a gentle pace, allowing your arms to flow in time with your legs. Become aware of your feet making contact with the earth as the foot rolls forward on to the ball and then lifts and travels through the air allowing the other foot to repeat the cycle. Notice the sensations in your joints as your foot is on the ground and then travelling through the air, and let the joints be relaxed, letting go of any tension. And notice your calf muscles as you're walking and connect with them but allow them to be relaxed and then become aware of your hips and abdomen, chest and shoulders, and head.

Keeping the whole focus of your body in your awareness, try to remain silent throughout the walk and bring your attention to your ears and listen to what you can hear. See if you can pick up the sounds of nature, any sound that is not man-made. Keep your awareness in your body and through your ears. And look at anything natural like birds or clouds or a blade of grass. Each time the mind wanders just escort your attention back to the soles of your feet and your arms swaying alongside and the surrounding sounds and look at the nature that is surrounding you with your eyes.

AFFIRMATIONS

I can create happiness in my life today.

My resilience and self-love will carry me through all adversity.

I am safe and I can trust myself.

I deserve to live a joyful and happy life.

PART THREE

Final
Thoughts

The Gifts of Recovery

Not enough is written about the amazing things that happen when we delve deep and reconcile old patterns of behaviour. Not enough is said about the peace that comes with letting out our sorrow and pain. We don't flag up the amazing results we see when we stand up for ourselves with the conviction of an adult who's recovered. These things must be said so that people who are still suffering understand the transformations that are possible.

Like many others I have fully recovered from depression and my aim in this book is to share with you the secrets of the gift of recovery that awaits you too. These gifts are waiting for you even if right now you feel you are lost in the fog. I hope the light from my torch will help guide you home.

Authenticity

By throwing off the shackles of who we think we should be, and embracing new beliefs, ideas and thoughts, miracles happen. When we do the real work of recovery, we change from the people we thought we were to the person we really are. Authenticity is the result. What this means is having the courage:

- To say what we think
- To believe in what we say
- To choose to be honest to others
- No longer to feel ashamed of our real selves
- To recognize that we struggle but are OK with that
- To know that we're imperfect and embrace that

- To set our own boundaries and take good care of ourselves
- To commit to a new life of real 'work' – the work that heals us

Being authentic is not the easy choice but is the purest gift that comes with recovery from depression. Others may struggle to come to terms with our real self if only because we've spent so much time in hiding. To be able to say 'I feel lousy' without shame or guilt is a miracle. It's also healing because we no longer have to hide our predicament from ourselves. Practising mindfulness meditations helps us to accept our inner world and build our resilience. In building our inner resources we also build our ability to become more open. The two pillars of authenticity are acceptance and resilience. Once these are in place, everything else will follow.

The re-emergence of our dreams

Once you're on the road to recovery you will discover your stifled dreams begin to surface. This signals the re-emergence of your real self because you are moving away from the person you thought you had to be. Hopes and desires return, often from years ago. Perhaps you will discover that you have taken up a career that you thought you *should*, but it turns out to be not what you actually wanted to do. Recovery from depression gives us the opportunity to revisit past dreams and put new goals in place. Perhaps you wanted to be a writer or a musician but became a doctor instead. You may even have climbed to the top of your game because you were good, but it wasn't really you.

The idea of realizing your dreams may be frightening but by staying with your mindful practice you can dissolve the fear quickly and learn to embrace this new freedom. It's important to take your hopes and desires seriously because they are as much a part of your spiritual recovery as everything else. We honour the inner child by acknowledging that there are more paths to walk to fulfil our creativity.

We can let other people go

For me, the greatest gift of recovery was the freedom of not expecting others to fix me. Having spent many years being sick and tired of being sick and tired, becoming obsessed with others, being responsible for their feelings, feeling guilty for standing up for myself, making pleas and threats, becoming rigid or possessive and many other traits, the joy of not behaving this way is profound freedom. I learnt to see others as separate from me, that they were able to take care of themselves, and that it's not appropriate for them to take care of me. That helped me to let them go. Once that happened I could begin to have real, authentic, intimate and fulfilling relationships. Life starts here!

Feelings no longer frighten us

Staying with our feelings is probably the hardest thing for anyone suffering from depression to do. Most of us invest a lot of energy trying to keep them away! Unless, that is, we've been so depressed that we've had no choice but to face them. This is a real gift. Once we meet our feelings and embrace them through our mindfulness practice, we see deeply into them. We learn that they come and go and that ultimately they can't harm us. Coming to terms with our feelings is the compassion we need to heal. The ritual of being aware of our feelings, embracing them and accepting them relieves the mind of the desperation of trying to get rid of them.

Our perception shifts from obsessing about feelings to watching them like clouds moving across the sky. They no longer pose themselves as a problem or a threat. The world holds much more promise if we release our fears about our feelings. Mindfulness will help us do this.

We learn to have fun again

It's time to let the inner child out and have fun. Woody Allen said 'Most of the time I don't have much fun. The rest of the time I don't have fun at all.' How many of us identify with that? It's so easy to forget that we're supposed to have fun – yes, even as adults! It will happen as part of the recovery process. We forget to be 'grown up' all the time and let our squealy, shouty, happy child out to play. It really does happen.

Peace of mind

Practising mindfulness slows down the racing thoughts until they come to a complete stop. What's left? Peace of mind. What next? Bliss. Harmony. Meaning. Life purpose.

> *Here's a summary of the whole book in one paragraph*
> By practising mindfulness in our everyday life, our every waking hour down to our moment to moment existence, we bring our full attention to bear on the depression and our associated negative emotions. This halts the cycle of 'obsessive thoughts' which manifest into 'painful feelings'. Our sustained attention quickly dissolves the depression *in this moment* and we feel a sense of peace. Because whatever we focus on grows, if we maintain our attention on our inner body, rather than our mind, we increase our inner peace. We learn to think only when necessary and rest in our inner body when we're done thinking. We can use the depression and our negative feelings to fuel the fire of awareness and peace.

How to Get Help

All of us need help. No one can recover from depression alone. You may well have a strong circle of friends or a partner who can help by listening and being supportive. However, you may also need to speak to someone outside of your circle. But where do you find this help?

There are two main streams of help: first, professionals who understand the depths of depression and, second, those in a similar situation. The fastest route to beating depression is to get assistance from those who understand your feelings and this is where a good counsellor can help. Getting support from others who have been through similar experiences to you will help you feel much less isolated.

Counselling or therapy

Finding one person to be available to you can be a lifeline. I know that I couldn't have got back on my feet without some personal help. I tried several counsellors/therapists until I found someone who totally understood that I had to share everything about me and have it accepted before I was ready to move forwards. Although it took some time, I was able to beat depression *much faster* than if I'd been on my own. In fact, I'm not sure I'd have beaten it at all without the help from other people.

When anyone begins to look for help it can seem confusing as to who's out there. Here's a quick guide:

The distinct difference between counselling and therapy is that counselling generally means relatively brief treatment that is focused most upon behaviour, often targeting a particular symptom or problematic situation and offering suggestions and advice for dealing with it. Therapy, on the other hand, is generally a longer-term treatment which focuses more on gaining insight into chronic physical and emotional problems. Its focus is on our thought processes and the way we see the world rather than specific problems.

Can I afford it?

The problem often isn't so much *which* help to get it's more a matter of cost. With counselling/therapy treatments being cut back from health services and long waits for free services, the onus is often on the individual to seek the help they need. Private treatment can be costly but it's worth knowing that many counsellors/therapists have a certain number of 'slots' each week to assist those on a low income. Also, there are charitable organizations that employ highly trained staff but charge low prices. Since it's important to get the support, asking around and researching local practitioners might bring you great success.

How do we know who's right for us?

When I was so depressed that I could hardly function I simply rang someone, showed up and collapsed. Sometimes it's like that. The first person I saw wasn't the right one. She would make a pot of tea, pour it out and smoke – I'm not joking – seven or eight cigarettes in the hour. I actually took up smoking to keep up with her. I stank when I left! She said nothing, gave me no feedback, just smiled or glanced down. Or nodded. Still, at least I'd made a start on getting help. The people I saw after her gradually got better until I found someone who really understood the nature of my depression. Once I found her, the change in me was dramatic and swift.

You won't know who's right for you until you try them out. It's a personal thing which comes down to getting along with someone. There's no shame in abandoning a therapist if it doesn't feel right. Building a trusting relationship is the key to making it work. If you don't feel safe, it won't work. Check out their credentials and make sure they have appropriate training.

My advice is to trust your own instincts. I believe that we find the right person for us at the right time. Even though I had a poor experience to start with, I was pretty 'off the wall' myself and might have found a highly trained therapist a 'bit of a bore' or going too slowly for me. I may not have been able to handle their gentleness or willingness never to judge me and to be there always. Who knows? It's a journey with no end and we meet extraordinary people along the way. There is a list of accredited organizations at the end of this book I can recommend you contact if you want to find professional help. Finding someone registered with a professional body is a safeguard, though that doesn't mean you will automatically have someone really, really good. A therapist or counsellor is only as good as their own journey, but having someone recognized by a professional body at least gives you recourse if it goes wrong. It's not likely that you will ever need it but having this recourse available is a step towards looking after yourself.

Peer support

Research shows that positive peer support contributes to us getting better quicker, dealing with stress more effectively and helping to increase our self-esteem. By reaching out to others and letting them see who we are we can build blocks of healing. It's the intimacy that can help us get better because it's often the difficulty we have in relationships that got us depressed in the first place.

The best known peer-support groups are the 12-step groups and they are found all around the world. Millions of people attend 12-step meetings every day. They are an underground movement that operates in the dark halls of churches and community centres. If you were wondering where depressed people go to get help, that's where they go. More information is below.

There are many, many other support groups that run throughout the country for a range of illnesses, disorders, or difficult social or personal situations. Don't dismiss these groups as sources of support. Sometimes they are a brilliant resource to get us opening up to others and telling our story. It's often easier to share about outside issues than our inner world and that might be good enough for the moment. The love that comes back is just what we need.

The 12-step groups

Originally proposed by as a method of recovery from alcoholism, 12-step groups started with Alcoholics Anonymous (AA) and hold meetings which are guided by a set of principles outlining a course of action for recovery from addiction, compulsion, or other behavioural problems. These groups are run by members, with no professional facilitators involved. The method was adapted and became the foundation of many other 12-step programmes.

Anyone who suffers from depression usually acts out other behaviours to help manage the depressive symptoms. As an example, how many of us turn to beer after a day's work to 'relax'? When the beer becomes two or five or we can't stop drinking at all, we have a problem. Some of us may have turned to gambling or shopping or recreational drugs to help us manage uncomfortable feelings, after all we're human! But when these behaviours become a problem in themselves, and we want to stop, we might find it hard to do so alone. This is where 12-step groups come into their own.

I spent a lot of time in WA (Workaholics Anonymous) and ACA (Adult Children of Alcoholics) because they fitted my behaviour. My compulsions were twofold: to work until I dropped (kept me from my pain) and to be focused on other people and their needs (and I lost my own identity in the process). By attending these two groups I found an incredible support system which played a big part in my recovery. I spent the first year, however, sitting on my own with 'piss off' slapped across my forehead because I was so insecure. But that gradually wore off and I was able to connect with other like-minded people who wanted more from life. These meetings are anonymous and only cost a small donation. There are millions around the world. Don't let the seedy halls put you off; they always take place in low-rent venues. If you need support it's worth checking them out.

Below is a list of the most common 12-step groups. A quick web search on any of these will give you the nearest group to you:

- AA – Alcoholics Anonymous
- ACA – Adult Children of Alcoholics
- Al-Anon/Alateen – for friends and family members of alcoholics
- CA – Cocaine Anonymous
- CLA – Clutterers Anonymous
- CMA – Crystal Meth Anonymous
- Co-Anon – for friends and family of addicts
- CoDA – Co-Dependents Anonymous, for people working to end patterns of dysfunctional relationships and develop functional and healthy relationships
- COSA – formerly Codependents of Sex Addicts
- COSLAA – CoSex and Love Addicts Anonymous
- DA – Debtors Anonymous
- EA – Emotions Anonymous, for recovery from mental and emotional illness
- FA – Families Anonymous, for relatives and friends of addicts
- FA – Food Addicts in Recovery Anonymous
- FAA – Food Addicts Anonymous
- GA – Gamblers Anonymous
- Gam-Anon/Gam-A-Teen – for friends and family members of problem gamblers
- HA – Heroin Anonymous
- MA – Marijuana Anonymous
- NA – Narcotics Anonymous
- NAIL – Neurotics Anonymous, for recovery from mental and emotional illness
- Nar-Anon – for friends and family members of addicts

- NicA – Nicotine Anonymous
- OA – Overeaters Anonymous
- OLGA – Online Gamers Anonymous
- PA – Pills Anonymous, for recovery from prescription pill addiction.
- SA – Sexaholics Anonymous
- SA – Smokers Anonymous
- SAA – Sex Addicts Anonymous
- SCA – Sexual Compulsives Anonymous
- SIA – Survivors of Incest Anonymous
- SLAA – Sex and Love Addicts Anonymous
- UA – Underearners Anonymous
- WA – Workaholics Anonymous

Helplines

Many organizations have websites and helplines ready to offer support and advice if you need to speak to someone. These include:

Rethink Mental Illness

Support and advice for people living with mental illness.
0300 5000 927 www.rethink.org

Depression Alliance

Charity for sufferers of depression. Has a network of self-help groups.
www.depressionalliance.org

CALM

CALM is the Campaign Against Living Miserably, for men aged 15–35.
www.thecalmzone.net

MDF: the bipolar organization

A charity helping people living with manic depression or bipolar disorder.
www.mdf.org.uk

Samaritans

Confidential support for people experiencing feelings of distress or despair.

08457 90 90 90 (24-hours) www.samaritans.org.uk

Sane

Charity offering support and carrying out research into mental illness.

0845 767 8000 (daily, 6pm–11pm) www.sane.org.uk

Mind

Promotes the views and needs of people with mental health problems.

0300 123 3393 www.mind.org.uk

The Mental Health Foundation

Provides information and support for anyone with mental health problems or learning disabilities.

www.mentalhealth.org.uk

Professional bodies

Here are some professional bodies and information about counsellors and therapists registered with these organizations.

British Association for Behavioural and Cognitive Psychotherapies

BABCP is the lead organization for Cognitive Behavioural Therapy in the UK. Membership is open to anyone with an interest in the practice, theory or development of CBT. BABCP also provides accreditation for CBT therapists.

www.babcp.com

British Association for Counselling and Psychotherapy

BACP is one of the UK's largest professional bodies for counselling and psychotherapy. Accredited Members have achieved a substantial level of training and experience approved by the Association.

193

All members are bound by a Code of Ethics & Practice and a Complaints Procedure.

www,bacp.co.uk

British Psychoanalytic Council

BPC is a professional association, representing the profession of psychoanalytic and psychodynamic psychotherapy. BPC registrants are governed by a Code of Ethics, a policy of Continuing Professional Development, a statement on confidentiality and a complaints procedure. The BPC is a Member Society of the European Federation for Psychoanalytic Psychotherapy in the Public Sector (EFPP).

www.psychoanalytic-council.org

College of Sexual and Relationship Therapists

COSRT members offer a range of treatments encompassing sex therapy, psychosexual therapy and relationship therapy. COSRT has a Code of Ethics and Principles of Good Practice for members, and a Complaints Procedure.

www.cosrt.org.uk

Counselling & Psychotherapy in Scotland

COSCA is the professional body for counselling and psycho-therapy in Scotland, and seeks to advance all forms of counselling and psychotherapy and the use of counselling skills by promoting best practice and through the delivery of a range of sustainable services.

www.cosca.org.uk

Federation of Drug & Alcohol Professionals

FDAP is the professional body for the substance-use field and works to help improve standards of practice across the sector.

www.fdap.org.uk

Health and Care Professions Council

HCPC is a UK-wide health regulator, responsible for the statutory regulation of 15 different professions. Registration with the HCPC means that a health professional has met national standards for their professional training, performance and conduct.

www.hpc-uk.org

Irish Association for Counselling and Psychotherapy

IACP was established in 1981 in order to develop and maintain professional standards of excellence in the counselling and psychotherapy profession. All members of the IACP are required to abide by the association's Code of Ethics & Practice and a Complaints Procedure.

www.irish-counselling.ie

The National Counselling Society

NCS was set-up in the late nineties by a group of counsellors, psychotherapists and hypnotherapists in a bid to support and promote counselling, and to protect the best interest of counselling clients.

www.nationalcounsellingsociety.org

United Kingdom Council for Psychotherapy

UKCP exists to promote and maintain the profession of psychotherapy and the highest standards in the practice of psychotherapy throughout the United Kingdom. Members must also adhere to approved Codes of Ethics and Practice and be accountable to UKCP Complaints and Appeals Procedures.

www psychotherapy.org.uk

UK Association of Humanistic Psychology Practitioners

UKAHPP is a national accrediting organization for all those who apply the theories of Humanistic Psychology in their work. The UKAHPP is an independent member organization of the UKCP and the UK Register of Counsellors.

www.ahpp.org